C000101979

On Eagle's Wings

Also by Lord Martin Cecil

BEING WHERE YOU ARE
AS OF A TRUMPET
MEDITATIONS ON THE LORD'S PRAYER

ON EAGLE'S WINGS

LORD MARTIN CECIL

MITRE PRESS
52 LINCOLN'S INN FIELDS · LONDON

© LORD MARTIN CECIL, 1977

The Mitre Press (Fudge & Co. Ltd.),
52 Lincoln's Inn Fields, London WC2A 3NW

SBN 7051 0257 2 (hard-back)
SBN 7051 0258 0 (paper-back)

Made and printed in Great Britain by
Cox & Wyman Ltd.,
London, Reading and Fakenham

Contents

Introduction

On Eagle's Wings is a sequel to a similar book published in 1974 under the title *Being Where You Are*. The composition of both is of an identical nature and, to be understood and enjoyed, should be read as though the words were being spoken, which indeed they originally were. The uninterrupted flow of the language allows the real meaning to become apparent.

Each chapter of *On Eagle's Wings* is a spontaneous address, tape-recorded at the time and subsequently transcribed and titled. While many subjects were covered, the manner of presentation and the wording was of such a nature as to be appropriate for the particular audience. For this reason some religious terms, mostly of the Christian variety, were used from time to time. The language is not the point. No one need be hung up on the wording. It is the spirit and substance of what is being said that carries the weight.

MARTIN CECIL

The Spiritual Expression of Life

Do you think that for a few moments we could set on one side our human concerns and affairs so as to release us into a realm of consideration of larger proportions? I am not suggesting that we should become involved in imaginary flights of fancy; it will only be imagination to the extent that we have had no real conscious experience of the reality which may be brought to point. But we cannot understand, we cannot encompass what is required, if we remain wrapped up in our own personal feelings and immediate experiences. It seems to take quite a strong compulsion of some kind to move people away from the immediate affairs, but you should be sufficiently resilient to be able to do so.

Most people have an awareness that there is a vast universe all around us, and while there may be a sensing of the unitary nature of the universe, the human mind cannot really encompass or comprehend what that wholeness is. There is a recognition of the unitary nature of various parts of the universe as they have come within the range of human awareness. For instance, a galaxy: here is a system of star systems which evidently have relatedness, in the galaxy system, to each other. It may not be seen what that relatedness actually is but at least the galaxy appears, from external observation, to be a unit. This solar system in which we are is a part of what has been referred to as the Milky Way system, a particular galaxy; and, of course, there is a recognition of the unitary nature of the solar system itself. This is more easily observed as being a little system interrelated; however, it is apparent that through all this vastness there is a state of being in operation.

The universe is operational. We see this operation in effect quite close to us, of course. Whatever it is that produces the operational

9

state of the universe also produces our operational state, because individually we are operational entities. Something compels the operation. The results of that operation can be observed and various theories about it postulated, various laws relating to this operation can be defined mathematically perhaps; but all this is in reference to the evidence of the operation. Why it is that way is an unknown quantity. Where there is a result, however, there is a cause. The cause, whatever it really is, springs from a realm which in one sense could be said to be nonexistent. Anything that does not find itself included in the realm of our observations tends to be looked upon as nonexistent. But the operational cause of the great universe and of the minutest part of it has been referred to by using the word *God*, but God has remained unknown because He cannot be found as God by examining the operational universe. But the very fact that the universe is operational actually reveals God.

The operational power, we could call it, the means by which the operation occurs, may be indicated by using the word *life*. There is evidence of this universal operational power because the universe operates and all its parts operate. In those parts which are relatively closer to us we can see something of the coordinated pattern. Coming right down to the state of affairs here on earth, nowadays they speak of the ecosystem. The operational power is at work throughout the whole universe. Because it is one system, a unitary system, a state of wholeness, it may be recognized quite easily that it is the same power which is at work. If we do define this working power as life, then we immediately recognize that life is inherent in the whole universe. Human beings have been investigating to try to find when life started. Life didn't start: it always is. Of course, usually the investigation relates to what has occurred here on the surface of this planet, but what has occurred here on the surface of this planet is merely an incident, a small incident, in the total operation of life which maintains the universal system. So life didn't start here. Life is already present everywhere by reason of the fact that everything is operational.

We have referred to a point, under the definition that it has position but no magnitude. This has provided a rather apt although limited definition of God, because insofar as the dimensional state which we experience is concerned God has no dimensions. Yet God has position, because life is operational throughout the universe. You could say He has universal position; however, by reason of the fact of the universe it is evident that what God is has in this fashion been given magnitude – in the overall sense the magnitude of the universe, however vast that might prove to be. The universe gives evidence of the reality of God, providing magnitude to that reality. As we have noted before, there is reference, for instance in the Psalms of the Old Testament, to the importance of magnifying the Lord.

Life is born into the dimensional universe. We note that the quality, the character, of life is naturally determined by the parents of life. Life is fathered by love and mothered by truth; the heredity of life, then, is love and truth. This is the nature of life when it is born. It is born out of a realm – and this seems to be a contradiction in words – of no magnitude. Someone may say, 'Well, then, how could it be a realm?' We have to use words. It is born out of a pneumatomenal state into a phenomenal state. In the phenomenal state the results of that birth can be observed. We have a certain experience ourselves of being alive, but that doesn't acquaint us with life in a way which would enable us to isolate and define it. We experience the results of its presence, of the fact that it has been born into this phenomenal world and specifically, insofar as we individually are concerned, into our phenomenal bodies. So life is present throughout the whole universe; there is nowhere in the universe where life is not. So the question, 'When did life start?', is a silly question. When did it start? or how did it start? It didn't; it is. Life, then, is the immediate contact with the ground of all being.

When talking about the galaxies they are sometimes referred to as island universes. This is a rather interesting description because we may gain something of an understanding of the nature of things by considering islands as they appear here on earth. It seems as though the galaxies are separated from each other by immense distances in space. If we come down to earth, then we may look at the Hawaiian Islands, for instance, and see several thousand miles of Pacific Ocean between this North American continent and those islands. The appearance is that they are separated from this continent by a vast distance of ocean, but we very well know that in fact both this con-

tinent and those islands are connected to the same earth; they are all
part of one thing and it is only an appearance that there is a separation of ocean. We do not deny the fact of the ocean, but at the
same time we know that the Hawaiian Islands would not be there if
they were not connected to the earth, and neither would this continent. Incidentally, of course, those islands appeared because of volcanic eruption, and the substance of the islands came up from the
depth of the earth; we also know that much of this continent has
seen volcanic eruptions. When those islands appeared above the surface of the ocean they were barren, but now there is much vegetation,
many forms of life, on those islands. Most of it came through the air.
Some of it came through the water. The human aspect came originally by water, but various plants and other forms of life were
brought by birds, for instance.

In any case, here we have an analogy which we can see in relationship to the island universes: they have a common ground of being.
The appearance is that they are separated by vast distances of space,
but they partake of a common source. All that has occurred, whether
on the surface of this planet or throughout the furthest reaches of the
universe, has been consequent upon life, upon this birth out of God.
The nature of life is the same everywhere. All life has the heredity of
love and truth, whether it is here or anywhere else. While there is a
vast variety of form through which life is revealed, the revelation is of
the same life; it does, however, indicate that inherently life is rich. It
isn't as though it were all the same thing in the sense of having no
variety; the differentiation of life is unlimited but what is being
differentiated is one thing.

Life operates the universe in this sense. Here is the operational
power. Being one thing, what unfolds through the universe is all one
thing. Seeing it in such tremendous terms and then coming down here
to this little planet and observing human beings running to and fro,
we may well see the utter futility of trying to control life, of trying to
use life for human purposes. We can try, all right, and human beings
have been doing so for ages, but the end result is futility, because it is
going to make no difference to what life is, nor is it going to prevent
the operation of life. Life is going to operate as life operates, not as
human beings think it ought to operate or as they would like it to

operate in their own experience. Of course, human beings may be generous and say, 'Well, it can operate out there any way it chooses but right here it is going to do it the way I want it to.'

In its operation life has created man, the physical form of man, both collectively and individually of course; there would be no collective form if it weren't for the individual ones. So, the form that we have has been created by this one power; there isn't any other. We have a physical body created by life and that physical body also has a consciousness created in the same way, because the consciousness of the body is the consciousness of the body; it wouldn't be there if it weren't for the fact that you have a physical body. The creative process didn't just come along and create consciousness here and there without regard to any physical manifestation. We have minds because we have bodies, but then, having a mind and a body operational because of life, insofar as human beings are concerned they have the ability to decide as to whether life shall remain in charge or as to whether they will become emotionally involved with other forms of life and on the basis of their emotions try to decide how they would like to have life operate through themselves. So, human beings feel what is occurring around them and then they try to use their minds to produce a continued experience of pleasing emotion: to be comfortable, to be happy, to be satisfied, to be fulfilled on the basis of how they feel. A person feels that he can use life in a manner that would be pleasing, so then he begins to think as to how he could arrange things, how he could manipulate life to produce what he imagines would be satisfactory in his own feeling experience, both physically and mentally. This is a futile endeavor, trying to manipulate life.

If the whole person were trying to manipulate life he would drop dead instantly. The manipulation, however, relates primarily to the conscious experience and to some areas of subconscious experience, most of which stem from earthly hereditary sources. Fortunately, there are other areas below the level of the conscious experience and beyond the hereditary experience which permit life to continue to be known in spite of the endeavors to manipulate it. There is that within a person which is still operated by life; the evidence of this is that we are still alive. If everything were taken away from the operation of life, then, obviously, what was left would be dead. This is the progressive movement of human experience: gradually more and more is taken away from the operation of life and given to the manipulation of human endeavor. Human beings are encouraged, after all, to try to make something out of life, which attitude obviously indicates that the person doesn't think that life is capable of making anything itself. Yet the fact is that it made the person; the evidence is there. And not only the person but the whole ecosystem insofar as this earth is concerned. And not only that but the planet itself. And not only the planet but the solar system of which it is a part. And not only the solar system of which it is a part but the whole galaxy. And not only the whole galaxy but the whole universe! Yet human beings imagine that they can somehow pervert life to their own uses, and it is also imagined that if they don't pervert life to their own uses life will be a drag. But the endeavor to manipulate life is futile and is proven to be futile. The manipulation, of course, takes many forms.

Most of the manipulation is designed to bring the individual to the experience of a futuristic goal; however, the fact of the matter is that life doesn't operate in the future; it operates now. If we want to consider goals, the only goal is now. There isn't any other goal but now; anything in the future is simply imagination. The goal could be said to be the experience of what life is now. Now, this is not the attitude of human beings who are manipulating life, because they are always anticipating a goal in the future. 'I am going to be educated now so that I may reach some goal in the future,' and people have these approaches where there is the expectation of experiencing meaning in the future. There is, as we have previously noted, a will to meaning in human beings. Everybody, consciously or unconsciously, is impelled toward the experience of meaning. But if that meaning is supposed to come on the basis of manipulating life, it will always be thought of as in the future, because it can never be experienced in the present. It can't be experienced in the present on the basis of manipulating life; therefore the whole operation in the human sense is futile, because the goal always must be in the future; it is always just beyond and beyond. 'When I graduate, then something or other,' and 'When I am able to function in the mature world, then something or other.' There is always a reaching for something that is ahead. It is imagined that there would be no movement if one weren't reaching for something ahead, but life isn't reaching for something ahead. Life is in the present moment; it is only in the present moment; it isn't anywhere else. Unless we are impelled by life in the present moment we do not experience the goal, which is the experience of life in the present moment. We may say in imagination, 'Well, if I experience life in the present moment it will lead to this and it will lead to that and it will lead to the other thing.' Maybe. Who knows? The reality is the experience of life in the present moment; there isn't any other.

So, the true goal is not experienced as a futuristic event: when such and such occurs, then ... This is vain and evil imagination, which establishes the wickedness of man in the earth. Yet how much do you function on this basis, on the basis of what you imagine you will be able to do when? That is imagination and it is futile. The question is, what is the experience now? The experience of the true nature of life now is the goal, but even that is projected into the future, isn't it? You find yourself saying, 'Well, how *will* that be known?' and immediately a person is back in the realm of imagination. It is known now. The meaning of life is known now or it isn't known. It never will be known; it is known now. What is it in the experience of a person that gives meaning to life? Life has meaning, but what is the person's experience of that meaning? Of course, he has to experience it to know it. It is not a matter of trying to imagine what it would be and then trying to catch up to the vision, because the experience is available now and can only be known now. This requires a change in the attitudes of human beings, of course, and there is a tendency to feel that it is all very difficult. It is only seemingly very difficult because the individual is all wrapped up in this unreal nonsense of trying to manipulate life. As long as that attempt is made he is living in an unreal state, a state that is only existent in his own imagination; it isn't the state that is. The state that is is the operation of life in the present moment.

Meaning in human experience – in all experience, as far as that is concerned, but it takes a peculiar form in human experience – the meaning of life is defined by the words *spiritual expression*. It is not defined by the satisfactory physical experience or the satisfactory mental experience; it is spiritual expression by reason of the fact of physical and mental experience. The fulfilment is not in the physical and mental experience but in the spiritual expression, but there could be no spiritual expression insofar as you are concerned if it were not for the fact of physical and mental expression; in other words, by reason of the fact that you have a body and a mind. But the body and the mind of themselves cannot find meaning. This is the human endeavor, and has been: to find meaning. 'I will have meaning when I go into business. I will have meaning when I get married. I will have meaning when I rise to high position in politics. I will have meaning when I run a particular race faster than anyone else has run it before.' Nonsense, because the fact of the matter is that the meaning is present now, and it is not and never will be a futuristic thing. If it is not known now it never will be known. So the chase after meaning, after this goal, which is the goal that human beings sense, is always futile if it is projected into the future; and you have to examine yourselves quite carefully to see that you are not projecting it into the future, because automatically you do it. The state has been of such long standing in human experience that nothing else, virtually, is known.

But life is still present, life is still operational; therefore it can be known; the nature of it, the quality of it, can be known. And it is known in spiritual expression. Spiritual expression is the nature of life and only in spiritual expression does the individual experience meaning. To the extent that spiritual expression is prevented the individual feels meaningless and therefore he thinks he must project meaning into the future. 'One day I will be meaningful, because now I am meaningless' – this is the attitude, isn't it? People would not want to project meaning into the future if they were feeling meaning and knowing the reality of meaning now. As long as it is projected into the future it is never experienced. In effect, a person is saying, 'I am now meaningless but I will be meaningful when such and such an occurrence appears.' But the occurrence which gives meaning is life, and life is now. When life is not manipulated but is allowed to express its meaning in spiritual expression through your body and mind, then you know meaning. You know meaning now and you may have the expectation of knowing meaning in all the nows that are yet to come, but you are no longer projecting meaning into the future. There are those, of course, who have felt so meaningless that they had to project their meaning to the point after death: 'When I am dead I will have meaning.' How ridiculous to say, 'Tomorrow I will have meaning.' It's exactly the same thing. Yet the idea of futuristic meaning is deeply embedded in the human consciousness. But it never comes; it is never experienced on that basis. Now is the time of meaning. In whatever spiritual expression appears through you now, inherent in that is your meaning, and inherent in that is fulfilment consequently, the true joy and satisfaction of living.

How to bring human beings down to the present moment where life is, to be willing to stop trying to manipulate, stop trying to make it serve body and mind? The only reason for the body and the mind is to give spiritual expression, and that is the meaning of life. Only in that experience does a person have meaning and know meaning for himself or herself. Why would it not then be the course of wisdom to be utterly concerned about what it means to give spiritual expression? But human beings are much more willing to set that on one side in favor of what they want, in favor of 'Well, it will make me feel good if I do this; I will enjoy that,' etc., and the individual goes in the direction where he thinks the goal is — but the goal is right here — instead of accepting life now and letting it find spiritual expression through body and mind. If this is the concern, then of course consideration is immediately given to the ways and the means by which the fulness of spiritual expression may appear in any given moment, that is all. There is the meaning.

The meaning of human beings is in their spiritual expression, the expression of spirit, the primary element of which is described by the word *life*. Expressing the qualities of life, the heredity of life, wouldn't that enable a person to live? Of course! This is life! Let's not try to qualify it by using the word *eternal*; it's life in the moment; there it is, the operational power of the whole universe from the greatest to the smallest. Let us be aligned with this power instead of trying to manipulate it.

One Life

We recognize what may well be called oneness. What this word really means seems, presently, to be beyond the comprehension of human minds. The experience indicated by the word *oneness* has not been known on earth for as long as human memory goes back. The idea has been present. People talk about the brotherhood of man, for instance; but this, in the human consciousness at least, is certainly not oneness – just what may be called brotherhood, a relationship between people. The reality of oneness is so far beyond any such concept that it bears little resemblance to the idea.

We say there is one God, one focus of all being. One of the evidences of the reality of this one God is seen in what is called life, life which permeates the whole universe, so that there is no such thing as the absence of life anywhere. To put it another way, there is no such thing as death. All the forms in the universe, whether physical forms or vibrational forms, are the forms of life, the evidences of this reality which is called life, which in turn is the evidence of love and truth; for love and truth are the true and natural characteristics of life. Love and truth in turn are the evidence of God, one God, one life, causing the universe to be one whole. Life springs forth through all the multitude of forms. That springing forth will depend upon the nature of the form, or the extent of the springing forth will depend upon that. But all forms, wherever found in the whole universe, are the evidence of life. Coming to this little planet, the forms of life on the surface of it are of a particular nature, and human beings are inclined to imagine that if they are not of this nature there is no evidence of life. The moon, for instance, would no doubt be looked upon as a dead form. It isn't, any more than the earth is a dead form. There is no such thing as a dead form, because the only reason that any form exists is by reason of life. All forms reveal the reality of life, which reveals the reality of God.

If we are hung up on the external form of things, we see a myriad different kinds of them, even from the standpoint of what human beings consider to be alive on the surface of this planet. How many forms are there from the mineral to man? A vast array, and yet life is one. It is not a different life made evident merely because the form is different. It is all the same life, but inherent in that life is what we speak of as truth, and truth may be seen as containing design and control. Love, the power of love, working through the design and control of truth, allows for the manifestation of life; and life permits the manifestation of form; but the design is not limited to one form, except as one might see the whole as one form, the total universe as one form. There are a myriad forms but one life and one God. To be identified with form is to be identified with something that by its very nature, its living nature, is changing. Human beings have lost themselves in the form, or the appearance of things, and have felt themselves to be separate from life, so that life could somehow be used for human purposes. This, of course, is an illusion in the sense that any such attempt brings the experience of the absence of life, because life is life and human beings can't change it; all they can do is change their own experience of it. If an individual tries to use life because he wishes to make pleasing forms, life proceeds in life's way and leaves him with the husk – a gradually increasing experience of the absence of life, until there is a complete absence in the person. That is called death, which is nothing, because life is everything. Life informs the whole universe. There is nothing outside of life. To speak of the absence of life, then, is to speak of nothing – there is no such thing. Now we can see this, perhaps, as being logically true, but our feelings probably don't agree. What we consider to be our experience keeps convincing us of the reality of death, but it has no reality because there is nothing other than life. Life cannot be absent; it is the nature of life to be present; it is the nature of God to be present. If we are convinced of the reality of the illusion, then we are in a sad way; and, as virtually all human beings are convinced of the illusion, all human beings are in a sad way.

But the reality of oneness is present, capable of being experienced.

In religious literature there is some indication of this: in the Bible for instance, and also in the Bhagavad-Gita. All is one. To know the identity of true being is to know oneness. If we don't know that, we experience separateness, which human beings do. Each person thinks of himself as a separate entity; and there is great anxiety, or has been, in the religious world of Christianity that somehow or other there may be assurance that this separate entity is going to be preserved. It's called a soul, a peculiar floundering entity that apparently is so important in the sight of God that it should be preserved at all costs. This soul is a concept of the human mind which doesn't really exist in reality. God is real, life is real, and the multitudinous differentiations of life are real. Does life need to be saved? Life is alive; that is its nature. If there is identification with life, life is known. If one maintains a position of separateness from life and tries to hang on to it, he will lose it. The true identity to be experienced by anyone is that of life — we might say a differentiated aspect of life peculiar to the individual, but life nonetheless. That's what it is, and life is eternally alive.

The universe itself is an eternal structure that gives evidence of the eternal nature of life. Of course, eternity is usually looked upon by human beings as being something of very long duration, but it really isn't, you know. Do you know what eternity is? The present moment, something that has no dimensions. It isn't length. It's a point which has position but no magnitude, and there is never any other point. It's impossible to get out of the present moment. It's known to be eternal when we learn to stay in it, but of course it's the human custom of long standing, being identified with the form of things, the changing form of things, to be all involved with the past and the future, to the detriment of the present. The only moment we can be alive is right now. Can you be alive yesterday? You may say, 'Well, I was alive yesterday.' But when you 'was alive yesterday' it was the present moment, wasn't it? It wasn't yesterday. You can't be alive yesterday and you can't be alive tomorrow; you can only be alive now. The one point of contact with life is in the present moment. Step out of the present moment too far and there is a complete absence of life; but, as I say, most human beings do not know how to live in the present moment. The present moment only has meaning to them in relationship to the past and the future; it apparently doesn't have any reality of itself. It's always seen relative to the past or the future in human consciousness. It is said of some people that they live in the past. Well, they're not living; they're dying. Others are always looking to the future for the experience, presumably, of more life. But they're dying, too, because all the life there is is present now. We don't need any more. We need to know the life that is; to live now, one with life.

In the New Testament of the Bible, according to the record there, Jesus indicated on several occasions that life is now. When speaking of the resurrection, for instance, those who were present at that time were looking to the future. It doesn't seem much different now, for many. They were looking to the future, but He said that now is when life may be experienced, because now is the only reality insofar as we are concerned. If we, individually, have reality we have it now. We have it now because of life, because of the real quality and nature of life, which reveals the quality and nature of God.

It is said that man was made in the image and likeness of God. This image and likeness is only possible of experience now. It is not something toward which human beings are evolving; for life is now. If we are identified with the form of things, then changes are occurring, certainly; and nothing is sure, apparently. In the funeral service they often say, 'In the midst of life we are in death,' or something of the sort – we may kick the bucket anytime! – if we're in luck we may be alive tomorrow. But we are lucky to be alive now, if you want to put it that way, because we still have the opportunity to accept identification, in the present moment, with the reality of life, which is the evidence of God. Would we not find ourselves in the image and likeness of God if that were done? This is not a popular thought with most people because they are enamored of their sense of separateness. 'My importance,' the individual is inclined to say, 'is based in the fact that I am a separate person. Just take a look at me, I'm the important one.' Will that person be important in a couple of hundred years' time? What will be important in a couple of hundred years' time? Life – it will still be present. Oh, of course, there are those who anticipate that it might be that all life would be obliterated from the surface of this planet. Maybe. Would that scotch life in the universe? Of course not. Life still is. Life doesn't come from somewhere. It didn't come from somewhere to be put here on earth somehow, in a little amoeba perhaps: 'Let's have a little piece of life and put it in this amoeba and then let her rip.' Then the amoeba will evolve and evolve and, lo and behold, a man! Do you think that's really the way it works? Of course not. Life is an inherent reality everywhere throughout the whole universe.

Let me state again that there is nowhere where life is not. Now here life is, and who's going to stop it from being now here? Certainly it is beyond the human ability. Human beings may separate forms from life; they have become rather expert in this, particularly their own personal forms – experts in dying. They have long experience, generation after generation, and each newborn child is taught as soon as possible how to die – not how to die in a gentlemanly fashion but just how to die, how to follow out the ideas and concepts popular in human consciousness, so as to end up dead. Everybody is trained in this; all of us have been, and with so much training we become experts. And in this regard, in this one regard, human beings have been immensely successful; they know all the tricks of dying. But to live, what would that be? To have the experience of a living soul, what would that be? For a soul is formed of the dust of the ground, a physical body with a capacity of consciousness. That's the human soul. It has the experience of being the dying soul, so in this sense it could be said that that soul needs saving; it needs to become a living soul in experience, rather than a dying soul in experience.

Strange, isn't it, how human beings die all their lives, and when the soul is dead, then they say, 'Well, save it.' But the opportunity for its salvation has been present continuously while it was alive, because life was present. When life is absent the form no longer exists. Of course, even in this human beings become somewhat expert in embalming, so as to preserve the form. But what's the use? It's of no value. It's much more valuable as fertilizer, participating in the cycles of life. The soul is offered life all its days, but few there be who accept it. It is, normally, in the human view at least, rejected because it is considered to be normal to die. All kinds of peculiar arguments arise if it is suggested that human beings were not created to die. 'Well, wouldn't the world become a pretty crowded place?' It's become a pretty crowded place even though human beings die, and maybe it is because they die that it has become a crowded place. There's something that bears a little thought. If they were living, if life were in control, then it is conceivable that human beings would not breed so promiscuously.

It is possible that there is a design, not only possible but the fact. The design is an aspect of truth, and truth is present in life. In life is contained all that is necessary to the right manifestation of itself throughout the whole universe, and incidentally in what is called man. I don't think that's such a big thing, do you, in view of what may be present in the total universe. Life is capable of operating man, whereas man is totally incapable of operating himself. Presumably we came to that awareness ourselves, in relationship to ourselves, or we would have no interest in turning toward the experience of life. Most people imagine they have the experience of life; the only thing they think they don't have is sufficient expertise in manipulating it so as to produce something that is pleasing and more lasting than it proves to be. So everybody's off on this kick. But here is life, patient, patient with human beings; otherwise they could hardly have continued to exist this long on the face of this earth. And we have come to an awareness that there is no such thing as the absence of life, but we do not yet have an adequate experience of that truth. Right? To know it with one's mind doesn't get the job done. It is necessary to allow the sense of identity to emerge out of the form into what gives the form meaning, which is life. When there is no more life in the specific human sense in the human body, that body has no more meaning. The only meaning that a human body has is the meaning that is given to it by life, and inherent in that life is all that is essential for the fulness of meaning to come out through that human body into expression on earth, thereby revealing something in the image and likeness of God.

I had a letter the other day from a lady who was somewhat troubled because she felt, possibly, that what was being offered through this ministry was in conflict with a certain passage in one of the gospels. I would read the passage:

'Then if any man shall say unto you, Lo, here is Christ, or there; believe it not.

'For there shall arise false Christs, and false prophets, and shall shew great signs and wonders; insomuch that, if it were possible, they shall deceive the very elect.

'Behold, I have told you before.

'Wherefore if they shall say unto you, Behold, he is in the desert; go not forth: behold, he is in the secret chambers; believe it not.'

There is a vast difference between a self-centered human being making claims for himself and for what he teaches, and the true uninhibited expression of the reality of life through a human form. This distinction, of course, has been recognized to some extent by those who call themselves Christians when they have looked at Jesus; for they say, 'Here was the Son of God.' Here was a form, a human form on earth, through which the divine was made manifest, or, as we are putting it now, through which life, the reality of life, was revealed. That is one thing. But human beings who insist upon their human state, their limited state, and then purport to be in position to lead others to the understanding of the truth, is what was being spoken of here through the lips of Jesus. And look where you will, on the face of the whole earth, where can you find those who are not functioning on this basis, who are not insisting upon being merely human, but claiming, nevertheless, to be able to direct affairs – the affairs of the individual life, or the affairs of the nation, or the affairs of the world – as they should be directed? It becomes more and more obvious that things are not being directed as they should be directed, but still human beings claim the ability to do it.

This is an attempt to be as God. That was the fall, so called, wasn't it? – the reason why man has become a dying soul instead of a living soul. He is so afraid of losing his precious useless identity as a human separate from other humans. He wants to rise up and be mighty, to continue to have self-importance. He that finds what he imagines life to be on this basis loses it, because it isn't life; it's an imitation. It's a human invention which people attempt to impose upon life and say to life, 'You operate this way through me, and you produce what I want.' Well, life is patient for threescore years and ten, or so, but eventually that's it, no more nonsense – for everyone. But life still remains – life, the evidence of God, completely capable of operating the creation that was called man, when that creation is willing to let it happen.

So we see how there are false Christs and false prophets every-where; for any human being, in whatever field of activity he may be engaged in, is false if he is trying to make life work according to the way he thinks it should work. And who doesn't? We have built up such good ideas about all this: it's very commendable if it works this way but it's not so commendable if you try to make it work that way — so may we all become very good according to someone's idea, in our endeavors to make life work the way we think it should. All kinds of systems have been devised in order to achieve success in this, so that we can all be good while defying life. Well, even if we achieve this we'll still die, because you can't defy life and continue to live.

Life operates as it should, and we discover what that is when we stop trying to impose our good ideas upon it. And let us not imagine that our good ideas are any better than someone else's bad ideas. It's all part of the same fruit which was forbidden on pain of death; it works! But life works too, if we will let it. And so we learn to let life work. Then the expression of life through human form brings forth accordingly an increase of life, so that we discover that it is true, individually speaking and collectively speaking: 'I am come that they might have life, and that they might have it more abundantly.' How can there be the increase of life in the experience of form on earth if life is defied? But human beings have taken that attitude: Life, you go the way I want you to go, or else. Well, of course, it's 'or else', because it won't go for very long the way we want it to go. It doesn't really go at all the way we want it to go. What happens is that we squeeze it out, out of our experience, and then we run to the doctor or someone else and say, 'Patch me up so that I can continue to try to make life obey me.' Blasphemy! But is it blasphemy to learn to obey life and let life reveal the nature of God on earth? That is what human beings called blasphemy in Jesus — the exact opposite of blas-phemy; everybody else was blaspheming.

So may we share the reality of the experience of life, because we are not concerned to preserve our precious humanness. This is what human beings think is so important: 'me'. Isn't that self-centered-ness? It certainly is. If we would forget 'me' we might remember the reality of life, the reality of life that springs forth in the present moment to be expressed according to its design, under the control of the spirit of God, to achieve what is necessary. Now, it isn't the achievement that gives meaning to life; life brings forth the achievement. The meaning is in life; the meaning is in God, in the true quality of being. Most people imagine that their meaning is in their achieving. 'I've had a rich life of achieving, therefore I've had meaning.' There's no meaning in that. Meaning is in being. When the meaning of being, of life, has been found, then all achieving has meaning; but no matter how much achieving there may seem to be, from the human standpoint, it is absolutely meaningless to the extent that there has not been the experience of being. You, as an individual, have meaning now in this present moment. You do not need to get meaning; it doesn't need to come to you from somewhere; it's there because life is there. That is your meaning. It is a reality now. You have the privilege of expressing it exactly as it is, without adjusting it to what you think it ought to be. Let it be what it is.

This requires a vast change in human attitudes and experience, certainly, and it's not all going to happen in a moment. But it happens when there is a willingness to let it happen, when there is an interest in letting it happen, when one begins to forget oneself in the human sense, relinquishing the attitude of self-preservation in this way. Why should we be preserved as dying souls? What would be the use? What would be the point? A dying soul needs to end up dead; that's fruition, that's fulfilment for a dying soul; get it out of the way. But why not permit the reality of the living soul to appear now? We don't have to evolve any; life is here now. Yes, some changes need to work out in our souls, in this form and its consciousness, certainly — changes need to work there — but that is not what we are. Our identity is in life, and when we find our identity in life we find that we are one because life is one.

I think, often, in considering the fact that properly there is a vast array of differentiations of God manifesting in form, it has somehow seemed that little pieces of God are snipped off and put in this form and in that form. No, it's one life. If my fingers come through the fingers of my other hand (demonstrating), they may seem like separate fingers, but they all stem from one hand. So is life. Life is one, and the Lord our God is one. The differentiations of life do not produce separateness, rightly. It only seems so when human beings claim life as though it were their own. Then they become separate, and proud in their separateness: 'Look at me, I'm very handsome,' or the lady says, 'I'm very beautiful, look at me.' Everybody looks at the forms, separate forms; everybody's separate. It's not so. It's one life. It seems to be separate when our identity is in the form, but it's all one when our identity is in the life which gives meaning to the form. And in that identity springs forth all that is necessary for right achieving – not achieving according to the ideas of men but achieving according to the purposes of God, which incidentally have very little to do with the ideas of men, although man's evidences of achieving, so called, may be used to advantage in the unfoldment of the purposes of God.

There is oneness in life. This is known when we are identified with life and relinquish our identification with the increasing absence of life. This latter is considered normal, isn't it? As we grow older there is an increasing absence of life: 'Poor me, I'm dying, but someone's going to help me to hang on a little longer.' Who's dying? Life? No! Well, why not find identity in life because this is the character of your experience? Then you live! And the fact that you live will be a blessing on earth, offering the increased experience of life to all who will receive it.

The True Stature of Man

Human beings have been thinking that they were thinking for quite a long time. On the basis of what they call thinking, various systems of knowledge have been developed. These systems have undergone revolutionary changes periodically, so that one particular pattern of knowledge was replaced by another. This always involved what might be describable as an earthquake, because human beings settle down into their crystallized states of consciousness and it seems to take the exertion of a certain amount of force to cause the crystallized state to break up. But thereafter, of course, it simply re-forms in a little different pattern. It is as though there was a crust on the surface of consciousness in human beings which gets stirred periodically and then re-forms.

Human experience is based, of course, in what we have described as self-centeredness – the projection of human beings to first place, as though there was nothing more important in the universe than human beings. Everything else that occurs near and far should, apparently, be subservient to the needs of human beings. With this outlook, everything is seen in a distorted way. Obviously, the universe is not, properly, subservient to human beings. The way people are on earth at the present time, it might be said that they are very small fry when we consider the total picture, scarcely discernible at all and carrying just about as much significance. Yet it has been said that man was originally made in the image and likeness of God. This should give him considerable stature, but in his self-centeredness he has lost his connection with God and consequently has lost his true stature. He sees everything through his self-centered eyes.

There is a description in the Book of Genesis as to what happened to the serpent that was in the tree in the garden. He landed up on his belly in the dust, and his diet was dust too. Now the serpent relates to the central nervous system in man, by which he finds his contact with the external world around him. In consequence of that contact he forms his various concepts with respect to that world. He generates a crust of consciousness. We are considering this from the standpoint of what has been occurring since self-centeredness set in. Man's consciousness has been hooked to externals and goes upon its belly in the dust, eating dust. In other words, man's awareness of his environment, and indeed of himself, is of a very lowly nature.

If we dust in our homes daily, the layer of dust which is constantly forming doesn't build up to any great depth; but if there is no one around to do the dusting it gets thicker, forming in a layer, but, even so, never a tremendously deep layer. If we consider the realm of man's activity here on the surface of this planet, it doesn't go very deep. He is related simply to the skin of the planet, a very thin layer of that skin, actually. Even his deepest oil wells scarcely penetrate into the skin, let alone through it. The vast majority of the planet is an unknown quantity, although various theories have been developed about it, based in different methods of indirect observation. But all that man really knows about is what is on the surface, related to the layer of dust. He does indeed, in his present consciousness, go upon his belly in the dust, and this is what he eats too, both literally and metaphorically. His present stature might well be compared to the lowly worm, and he has seen on occasion that he seems to occupy the position of the worm of the dust, certainly not the position of man.

Man, made in the image and likeness of God, should rightly have, presumably, considerable stature. He has been keenly aware of his lack of stature and has felt ashamed of it, but has thus far been unwilling to relinquish the things which keep him in that lowly state. Not only does he not know very much about anything but apparently he does not particularly want to know – this in spite of the idea that man has a voracious appetite for knowledge. But the only sort of knowledge in which he has an interest is the knowledge which enables him to maintain his self-centered state. Anything which seems to threaten his self-centered state he is inclined to reject out of hand; he doesn't want to know it. If he can discover those things which seem to support him in his self-centered state, then he points to that with pride, saying, 'Look, I am a seeker of the truth.' But that actually is the last thing which he seeks. All he has sought is a system of concepts which will sustain him in his self-centeredness, and this is what he calls knowledge. From time to time the system of knowledge which he has produced doesn't seem to be going to sustain him anymore in the manner to which he is accustomed, so it breaks up and he institutes a new one. He builds a new house; the old one fell into disrepair. He has done this over and over again down through the ages. Each new house has seemed to him to be a palace, a fit place of habitation for his self-centeredness.

In developing these various systems of knowledge, all he has utilized has been the dust of the ground, a very thin layer of physical substance. He may, standing in the dust, look outward beyond himself into the universe, but he has to use the serpent to do it, so he sees everything through the serpent's eyes, or through the worm's-eye view of the creature that goes on its belly in the dust. He stands in the dust and looks to the larger environment around him, seeing everything through those self-centered eyes; and he may also look in the opposite direction, inward to the very small, and he sees things there likewise. On the basis of this he develops what he calls his physical sciences, and the crust forms, forms within the scope of this thin layer of dust.

However, at the same time, he may indulge himself in the development of various philosophies. He moves into what may be called a metaphysical realm, something that is beyond the immediate experience of the dust. But this realm doesn't go very far either. It is perhaps comparable to the atmosphere around the earth. If we made a model of the earth the size of a soccer football, then the skin where man functions would be scarcely discernible insofar as thickness was concerned; likewise the surrounding atmosphere would hardly be discernible either. This is the little area of non-man's function in the self-centered state. It is interesting to look at some of the photographs of the earth that have been taken from space in the vicinity of the earth. What is mostly evident? Clouds. These clouds which are observable look as though they were right on the surface of the earth and, relatively speaking, that's where they are. From the standpoint of the worm's-eye view they may be thousands of feet up from the surface of the earth, but looking at them with a true perspective they are seen to be right on the surface of the earth. The atmosphere of this earth is a very thin skin too.

So the atmosphere and the dust are both relatively nothing, compared on the one hand to the body of the earth, on the other hand to the body of space. Yet it is within this range that human beings exist. Looking outward, they can't see anything except through this atmosphere; and looking in, they can't see anything except through this dust. The stature of man has been entirely lost, and insofar as the consciousness of man is concerned there is simply a serpent moving on its belly in the dust.

So, with respect to the dust itself there is the development of knowledge – what are called the physical sciences, for instance – and with respect to the atmosphere above, metaphysical philosophies. These philosophies have taken many different forms insofar as detail is concerned, but there is a general overall philosophy insofar as human beings are concerned. This philosophy centers in the state of human self-centeredness. This is naturally accepted as being the condition inevitably experienced by everyone all the time. But within the scope of this overall philosophy there have been various detailed concepts developed, systems of concept, purporting to describe what human beings imagine is the truth. Vast libraries of books have been written about such ideas, and there are proponents, of course, with respect to all of them: supporters, believers. However, all this relates to this very narrow range in which human beings exist in their self-centeredness, in the worm-of-the-dust consciousness.

Even in this state of consciousness there has been a recognition that the mind of man had far greater potential than is actually being used. I think perhaps it has been supposed that even in the greatest intellects only about ten percent of the mental capacity has been used. But this, of course, is from the worm's-eye view: only ten percent of the worm's-eye view is being used, let alone ten percent of the actual capacity.

If in our meditations we undertake to look beyond the worm's-eye view there are those who react in fear. To come out of the state of the worm looks as though it would cause a person to lose his sense of security – or any sense of security which he has, which probably isn't much anyway. But to lose that little bit is unthinkable to many, so there tends to be a more or less violent reaction on the part of the majority of human beings, based in not wanting to see the truth, and being desperately afraid of seeing the truth. This tendency is present in the self-centered nature of human beings. It's present in all of us. The vast majority of human beings won't even look in the right direction. They do everything in their power to avoid looking in the right direction, and if it seems as though they are being forced by circumstance to look in the right direction, they tend to react violently. True honesty, of course, compels a person to look. This being so, there is much evidence of very little honesty.

Those who do look, in spite of the general tendency which does not want to look, develop their philosophies on a basis which will allow them to maintain their sense of security, and consequently they only produce theories which permit the maintenance of self-centeredness. Now, this is true of the philosophies of men and the metaphysical concepts and systems which have been developed by them. Even in what is called Christianity, self-centeredness prevails. Human beings are taught to be deeply concerned about their souls, their own personal state: Maintain your self-centeredness at all costs, but we will provide a system which makes it seem as though the dust is being transcended. But it isn't, because whether one is pointed in the direction of the dust or pointed in the direction of the cloudy atmosphere, the person who is pointed in these directions remains the worm of the dust, remains in the self-centered condition; there is no change in the basic nature of human self-centeredness.

However, obviously, if human beings are ever to be restored to the state of man they must come out of this earthworm state. The necessity, then, is that something more be seen than is possible to the consciousness of the earthworm. However, in directing attention to that something more the tendency is to develop metaphysical concepts about it, so that the person may stay within the range of the dust and the immediate atmosphere, so to speak, may stay in the self-centered state. If, for instance, I begin to point to a larger sphere of understanding, there are those who, looking at it, claim that I am offering a new system of concepts; and there are others who look at what it is that I offer and develop a new system of concepts. In either case the real necessity of what needs to be experienced is overlooked. It certainly is not a matter of either seeming to accept a new system of concepts from me – I have no intention of offering one – or of developing a system of concepts from what I say (which is the only way, actually, that a system of concepts can be produced, because it is not what I offer). There must, however, be an introduction to an awareness of the real stature of man. If everything that is offered in this regard is translated, interpreted, on the basis of the worm's-eye view, then it merely becomes another philosophy, and human philosophies are no good; they're worthless.

We can either have a pattern of concepts about the dust or we can have a pattern of concepts about the atmosphere, as long as we remain in the worm state. That's all we can have, and there is nothing better about having a pattern of concepts concerning the atmosphere than having a pattern of concepts concerning the dust. Those who do develop patterns of concept with respect to the atmosphere usually look upon themselves as being above, more important, more valuable than those who merely have patterns of concept about the dust – but what's the difference? It's all the worm's-eye view; it's all the wormy state. So in our movement toward a new state of consciousness it isn't a move toward a new state in a system of concepts.

Man was created in the image and likeness of God, to have a stature which would be of God. The vast difference between present human experience and that, is incomprehensible to human beings. It's incomprehensible to the self-centered state of consciousness. However, if finally there is a certain willingness on the part of some to come out of that limited state and to find again the true stature of man, then there is a discernment of the real quality of that stature; but we cannot comprehend the real quality of that stature if we insist and persist on going upon our bellies in the dust. We must share a movement which allows us to come out of the realm of concept. We have taken note of the importance of actual experience, but the actual experience that is needed transcends the worm experience. We can't have the experience of the truth of man as long as we remain worms. This should be obvious, and yet how desperately human beings cling to the worm state; and if the door begins to be opened for the greater experience of the true stature of man, how very reluctant most people are to move through that door.

Let us for a moment consider something, do a little thinking without interpreting what begins to emerge in consciousness from the standpoint of the worm's view. In other words, let's not try to encompass what occurs in preestablished concepts. Let us not clothe the thinking process in our prejudices, so that we may let it be what it is, unencompassed by the self-centered concepts of human beings. We are not trying to grasp it so that we may take something and use it for our self-centered purposes, but are exhibiting a willingness to be restored to the true state of man – a state that presently is totally unknown, so we couldn't have a true concept about it! What's the point, then, of developing concepts about it? Let us let it be the actual experience which we know, and that experience unfolds to the extent that we have not tried to restrict it with our interpretations of it. The very moment we begin to develop a concept, we hem in what was happening and prevent it from happening in our own experience, so what might be looked upon as progress ceases. Of course, the progress is simply the unfoldment of potential, the unfoldment of the potential reality – potential to us as yet but already a reality in fact. This reality needs to emerge into our experience. It will not do so if we persistently, stubbornly, insist upon keeping our wormy state.

So, let us consider, and in this consideration I am trusting you not to form a system of concepts, a metaphysical system of some kind, a new philosophy. No doubt there are those who could easily do that, and those who might insist that this is what I am offering, but it isn't. We have to use words which have certain meanings in human consciousness. You have undergone a certain amount of change in this regard so that you have seen different meanings; but those different meanings that you see are now your present concepts, so do not restrict what is to unfold in your concepts of meaning. Allow yourselves to move with the spirit of what is occurring, because we are moving, in fact, to the state of man – who became man, when he was originally created, because the breath of life was breathed into his nostrils. The breath of life indicates spirit. His state of being man is absolutely dependent upon his experience of spirit, not upon his experience of mental concepts. The total experience of the worm of the dust relates to mental concepts. That is not man. Man's true experience relates to the breath of life, to spirit. He is not man until that is dominant in his experience. You can examine your own daily experience and recognize what is now dominant – mostly the forms which are taken by the dust of the ground, interpreted by your philosophical viewpoint, in other words the concepts which you have. This is the worm state, obviously. Man has tremendous stature when he is man, breathing the breath of life.

Now, we may look at the setting in which man finds himself on the surface of this planet. Presently that setting is simply a thin layer of dust and a thin layer of atmosphere. But there would be no possibility even of that if it were not for the fact, first of all, of the planet itself, what we call the earth, this rock moving in space. So we have one level here, the earthly level, about which, in the self-centered condition, man merely knows a little something of this skin of dust and atmosphere. Here is a very accurate portrayal of the state of the worm consciousness relative to the physical level of being, ignoring all the other levels of being but relative merely to the physical level of being. It's just this little thin layer. Human beings imagine that they know so much when what they know is scarcely discernible even in this first level of consideration where man rightly has responsibility. This relates to the total planet and actually includes also another body that is very closely related to this planet, namely the moon. Here we have the first level, the physical level, of being as it relates to man.

But this earth, with its moon, is not all alone in space. It has a relationship, an immediate relationship, to a number of other planets. In other words, here we have another level of being: the earthly level first of all, and then what we might call the planetary level, because the earth is part of a family of planets. This family of planets is interrelated and these interrelationships involve movement in a pattern of rhythm. Now, this immediate contact with the rhythmic movement which characterizes all things, through this system of planets, correlates with the mental level of consciousness in man. We have the earthly level, and the physical nature of man. The planetary level correlates with the mental nature of man. His mental nature, then, is getting a little larger than is the case with the worm!

And insofar as this planetary system is concerned, it does not exist all on its own. It has a relationship to what we call the sun. Now the sun is not merely that fiery orb that is observable when the sky is clear in the daytime. That is the core of what the sun actually is, but there is far more to the sun than this core. There is, for instance, what has been described as the solar magnetosphere. What the sun is extends through the planetary system and beyond. In other words, the planets are contained in the sun, even as the earth is contained in the planetary system.

So we have three levels here: the earthly level correlating with the physical nature of man, the planetary level correlating with the mental nature of man, and the solar level correlating with the spiritual expression nature of man. Here is a portrayal of what is properly the true nature of man in the external sense, in the manifest sense; and this is only part of man, isn't it? Man is more than that because of the breath of life. We may begin to see that beyond the solar system are other relationships, because the solar system does not exist just for itself. It is part of what is called the galaxy. But when we get beyond the solar system we get beyond the level of man in the external sense. We begin to find the correlation of man in the external sense with God in the internal sense.

Man is made in the image and likeness of God, and God is certainly not limited to this solar system, so we may go beyond the solar system and find the galaxy, one level beyond the solar system. We may go beyond that and find another level which relates to the system of galaxies. And we may go beyond the level of the system of galaxies to what is composed by those systems, the total universe. Here we have another three, internal levels, related to the internal nature of man, which is rightly the nature of God. So man, internally and externally, is made in the image and likeness of God. What vast stature is this! Just look at it, without forming concepts about it, because I think you would have great difficulty in doing that, and then look at the world, then look at human beings in their present state.

I have emphasized over and over again the vast changes that need to come in consciousness. Perhaps this outline will help you to understand how vast those changes really are, because we are not really worms burrowing around in the dust and that is all there is to us. If we try to maintain that state, no wonder we feel futile and frustrated. But if we feel that way it is because we ourselves have maintained that state. Of course, the worm looks around and accuses other worms of keeping him bound in this state, but that's not true at all. It has no basis in truth whatsoever. No one can keep anyone else in the wormy state. If we begin to see the vastness of what man really is, perhaps we may have a better comprehension of the nature of the irresistible force and what it is that is actually working and capable of restoring man. It isn't done by the efforts of the worms; it is done by the power of God, by this vast, almighty reality which encompasses the universe. Man is equipped to have a direct relationship to that. What a lowly state he has brought himself to, what a sad, insignificant condition, when the mightiness of what man really is is so tremendous.

Let us begin to sense once again the true nature of man and how it is related to the reality of God, and how in that relationship he finds himself as an essential element in the total operation of the universe. Clearly, for a person in the worm state of consciousness to develop some sort of a big head, a conceited view of himself as being so vastly important, is ridiculous. He isn't, in that state. He cannot comprehend the real nature of his importance until that state begins to be transcended because he is restored in his triune nature into the pattern, the design, of being. Then his mental processes correlate with the rhythms of the planetary state, the planetary level, Mazzaroth; and his spiritual expression with the solar level; and all based in his physical correlation not merely with the surface dust of the ground and the little area of atmosphere around the planet but with the earth itself and the total earth system. Then once again man begins to find himself with his true stature, made in the image and likeness of God.

Spontaneous Creation

I'm going to read most of an article from the September–October issue of this magazine called *Liberty*, which is a Seventh-Day Adventist publication. The article is by C. Mervyn Maxwell. It is, I presume, a continuing column entitled 'Insight'. The article itself is the answer to a question. Here is the question:

'There has been a lot of agitation in the wind lately to have creationism taught in public schools along with evolution. Tennessee has imposed a requirement. . . . Creation is a Bible doctrine. It's religion. I know that *Liberty* believes in creation, but shouldn't you be writing out against this new danger to the First Amendment? Religion should not be taught in public schools!'

Here is the answer:

'Suggesting an alternative hypothesis to evolution is not based entirely on a desire to teach religion in the public schools. It stems also from evidence that evolution is itself a "religion" – and one that is becoming increasingly untenable.

'In 1952, Harold Urey, a Nobel Prize winner, then of the University of Chicago, suggested that the first living cell may have come into existence as the result of a lightning flash searing its way through a smoggy primeval atmosphere composed of hydrogen, ammonia, water vapor, and methane. Not that the lightning could have alchemized a living cell at a single stroke; but it might, Dr. Urey proposed, have combined the gases into a number of different amino acids, and these, in turn, might have combined into proteins, and these, in their turn, might have combined themselves into the first living cell.

'In 1955, only three years later, one of Dr. Urey's students, Stanley Miller, mixed the four suggested ingredients in a bottle, discharged an electric spark through them for a week, and discovered on an-

38

alyzing the result that he had indeed brought about the formation of a number of different amino acids. What excitement! Man was about to demonstrate how life began.

'Or was he?

'Suppose the earth was at some time in the long-distant past draped with the necessary four-component atmosphere. Suppose the lightning did play through it with continuous abandon. Suppose amino acids by the million did rain down day after day from this agitated air into the primitive ocean below it. What are the chances that the right amino acids would have linked up with each other in the right order to form a protein molecule?

'The answer is fantastic!

'Amino acids occur in nature today in an almost infinite variety; and living protein molecules as we know them are highly complex. Unless every needed amino acid is present in a protein molecule, and located within it – in its own rightful place – the molecule simply cannot function properly, if at all.

'In 1964 Malcolm Dixon and Edwin Webb, on page 667 of their standard reference work, *Enzymes*, point out to their fellow evolutionists that – depending on the laws of chance arrangement alone – in order to get the needed amino acids close enough to form a given protein molecule there would be required a total volume of amino-acid solution equal to 10 to the power of 50 times the volume of the earth.

'The term 10 to the power of 50 indicates a one with fifty zeros after it. This means that only if you had a solution saturated with amino acids, in a quantity sufficient to fill a mixing bowl equal in capacity to one hundred quadrillion nonillion times the volume of our entire planet, could you hope that somewhere the correct association of amino acids would take place to form a single protein molecule!

'But we are dealing with the chance origin of a very simple protein. What are the odds in favor of the formation of a larger protein molecule such as hemoglobin?

'S. W. Fox and J. F. Foster have worked this out for us in their *Introduction to Protein Chemistry*, page 279. They have shown that only after the necessary amino acids had come together to form random protein molecules by the process described above, and only after these protein molecules had been formed in such a quantity that they filled a volume 10 to the power of 512 times the volume of our entire known universe (that is, 1 with 512 zeros after it times the volume of our entire known universe) packed solid, protein molecule to protein molecule, could we reasonably expect that just one hemoglobin molecule might form itself by luck alone!

'With each correct molecule occurring only once in an incomprehensible number of universes, just what really are the odds that enough of them would be found within the tiny space necessary for them to locate each other and link up to form a living cell?

'The answer to all intents and purposes is none. None at all.

'And yet the evolutionary hypothesis asks men of the twentieth century to believe that it did happen in the relatively shallow layer of moisture that wets a portion of our little earth's surface.

'Here, surely, is "blind faith"!

'Telling children that there is an alternative hypothesis involving a Master Intelligence is not so much religion as it is good sense.'

It has seemed incredible to the intellect of man that human beings could have been formed as a complete entity. There are various reasons for the incredulity. One of them, of course, might be that no one ever saw it done. Of course, it hasn't needed to be done, because we're here already. Obviously, the very fact that we are here already indicates an origin. Individually speaking we have some knowledge of the nature of the physical origin of ourselves as individual entities. This origin of which we are aware could be described as a spontaneous generation, could it not, proceeding from one cell, composed of its two halves, male and female, all the way to the completed adult body. This takes about twenty-one years, not a very long time if we take a look at the presumed length of time involved in the origins of the earth itself, or the solar system, or the universe. This has occurred within the scope of our own experience in a flash, hasn't it really? – in a time so short that it would, looking at it from the universal level, seem to be instantaneous.

I mention this because very often, when considering the creation of man by some supposed God, it is thought of as being an instantaneous experience, as though God said, 'Man, be,' and there man was. The way it is described in the Book of Genesis is that 'the Lord God formed man of the dust of the ground, and breathed into his nostrils the breath of life; and man became a living soul'. This does not particularly indicate an instantaneous experience; I wonder if there is, really, anything such as an instantaneous experience. We know well enough that even an atomic explosion is not an instantaneous experience. It is consequent upon what is called a chain reaction. In other words, there is a continuing cause and effect. It all happens very quickly, but it does take measurable time. And so it is with all creative processes. There is measurable time involved. From the point of the first cell in the mother's womb to the point of the baby's birth, there is the measurable time of nine months. A very brief moment in view of the idea proposed by the theory of evolution that the production of man has taken millions of years. Strangely enough, the production of man today, in the form of a babe at least, only takes nine months, seeming to indicate that vast periods of time may not really be necessary. It wasn't necessary insofar as we individually were concerned.

As has been noted, the idea of a spontaneous creation has seemed to be incredible partly because no one ever saw it happen. By the same token, no one ever saw a member of one species of animal, for instance, turn into a member of another species of animal. There are lots of things that haven't been seen, possibly because they never happened and possibly because they never happened within the scope of our own present observation. But there is evidence that miraculous things do happen, and I think just about the most miraculous thing within the scope of our own awareness is the production of our own physical bodies. Because it has been happening at such a proliferating rate over the years, and more especially in recent years, it is all taken very much for granted and no one thinks twice about it. But what a marvel! A spontaneous creation, formed of the dust of the ground.

Remembering that old story in the Book of Genesis as to how the Lord God took of the dust of the ground, this probably conjures up a picture in human consciousness of a big man, the Lord God (a large sculptor, shall we say?) who took some dust of the ground – He must have mixed it with a little water to get some clay – and then proceeded with His hands to mold it into the form of a man. We see this happening under the hands of a sculptor in these days, but of course it's a very surface manifestation, isn't it? There's nothing much inside that means anything. It may have the appearance of something externally, but to make a human being would take more than that. And in any case God didn't have any hands to do it with. So the picture, the imagination, is bound to be faulty; besides, anything that human beings look at they necessarily must observe through the coloration of their own consciousness. The consciousness of man contains a very great deal – I don't know how we might describe that very great deal; we could call it stuff – the vast majority of which has been brought forward out of the past to be included in the subconscious levels of man's mind, including what may well be called a race consciousness. There are all kinds of things present in the consciousness of human beings that have been brought forward out of the past. A little veneer has been added during the individual's sojourn thus far on this planet. But what has been added is proportionately a very small thing compared to what has been brought forward out of the hereditary past, so that the consciousness of man is full of a lot of stuff of which he has no direct awareness at all, but nevertheless it's there. And it is a potent and continuing influence in his outlook; his manner of thinking is largely governed by this, and his thoughts follow out certain well-established ruts, ruts based in the hereditary past.

Now, we needn't go back as far as the slime out of which he is supposed to have sprung in order to have a considerable hereditary past. Even if some of the factors contained in the theory of evolution were to be correct, then it is evident that man has been around quite a while. And it's interesting to note that discoveries that are made from time to time keep pushing back the time when man was an already established entity on earth, so that the need for some sort of a missing link which gets him connected up with more elementary species of creatures moves into the dim and distant past, even more than it has been.

In any case, there is this composition of the human consciousness. The human race has lived on earth for a considerable time and passed through many vicissitudes. Some of them, as we begin to recognize, were traumatic. Traumatic experiences tend to be buried. Even from the standpoint of psychological studies this is recognized to be so. If as individuals we have had difficult experiences along the way, we get them covered up as far as possible, but they're still present in consciousness, although hidden from direct awareness. Because these things are present in consciousness, they have an influence and they do determine the way we look at things and the way we behave, the way we handle things. Back in this subterranean pattern of consciousness there are some desperate fears and there is also a very firmly established pattern of shame, because even back beyond all this there is what might, I suppose, be called a thoroughly hidden memory of the truth in relationship to human experience, the truth of what it meant to be a living soul, formed of the dust of the ground with the breath of life breathed into the nostrils but a living soul rather than a dying soul.

Obviously there is a distinction here. We have very great experience presently, and out of the hereditary past, of what it means to be a dying soul, but apparently no experience of what it means to be a living soul. And yet, if the fact is that the origins of man relate to the experience of the living soul, then there is a memory, back under all this stuff, of the truth, and it is this truth that has an influence in the consciousness of man to cause him to feel ashamed. In other words, there is a faint, dim awareness of the truth in relationship to himself, of what it means to be a man or a woman – what the truth is in that regard, what a living soul really is. And he knows very well, in his own present experience, that he isn't what he ought to be, and consequently there is this sense of shame. But that too is deeply buried, because it is a painful thing to remember, and this pattern of guilt permeates the whole race consciousness of what should be man but isn't. The present human state, which certainly goes back in history quite some time, is the state of the dying soul, the state which is not man. And while human beings proudly refer to themselves as man, they don't know what they're talking about.

All this is present deep down in the consciousness of individual human beings. Part of that consciousness, as it goes to greater depths, is shared with others, and eventually it's shared with all others in the human race. In other words, there is a shared base in the experience of human consciousness that rises up to a point which is individually claimed, and we think of ourselves as being individuals. But there is much that is shared below the surface. And we can't very well, in this condition, help looking at things on the basis of this subterranean source of influence, so that what we see, what we observe, is not really what it seems to be. We have changed it in our own consciousness to suit ourselves, to suit ourselves in the sense that we don't really want to see the fact – the fact in relationship to our past – because it would be too painful. And so we have rather successfully blotted it out, and in place we have developed various theories, one of them the evolutionary theory, because this seems to be useful in persuading us that we needn't be ashamed. It wasn't our fault, you see. We're just the end of an evolutionary process which has brought us to this point, and all the things that have brought us to this point were really not our fault.

But we are a part of the body of mankind, and the fact of the matter is that mankind as such has indeed misbehaved, and that misbehavior has indeed brought its consequences. And those consequences, over an extended period of time, have been very painful. Even those rather minor consequences that we may observe by studying history as we know it have been rather painful, but these are quite minor compared to what has occurred in the history of mankind as such. As I say, there have been some very traumatic experiences back along the way, when only a very few human beings survived on earth. They did survive, of course, or we wouldn't be here, but the experiences were so awful that these things have been well hidden in the mass memory. Nevertheless they're present and they have their influence, and they cause us to be dishonest with ourselves, so that we avoid at all costs looking at what the facts really are, that looking beyond the facts of human history we might see the truth of man, the truth of man formed by the Lord God of the dust of the ground to become a living soul.

This is the true state of man, the way man was originally created. Because there is this in the far-distant heredity of man in the earthly sense, there is an inherent awareness with respect to each individual that he really should be more than he is. It is this awareness that has compelled human beings to strive; it has engendered their aspirations and ambitions, but all their striving, all their aspirations, all their ambitions, have been based in the dishonest view, in the distorted state of consciousness, which tries to blot out the facts involved. Obviously, one cannot come to an awareness of the real state of affairs if one is constantly trying to avoid looking at the facts. As I say, one of the ways of avoiding looking at those facts has been to develop the theory of evolution, for instance, and human beings have been searching everywhere to find support for this theory. But even though they have seemed to find some support for this theory, in their searching they have also found a lot that makes the theory untenable. This of course is unfortunate from the viewpoint of those who don't really want to face the facts. Human beings are afraid to face the facts, because those facts are so ghastly, it is such a terrible thing!

From the religious standpoint this has been described as the fact that man is a sinner, but this has got off on a tangent somehow, because it hasn't really allowed man to see how he is a sinner. It has really been assumed that he can't help it. Somebody misbehaved back along the way in some peculiar manner and subsequent generations were stuck with it. It never has been so. Each generation has had the opportunity of choosing for itself, and each generation has; but it has always been the same wrong choice. And of course, the wrong choice having originally been made and the results of that wrong choice having subsequently been experienced, building up in a number of sequential cycles to points of climax, cataclysmic experiences here on this planet, then there was more and more apparently to be buried, to be hidden, to be obscured, and more and more need to find a means so that it could be avoided being faced. All this is present in us as much as in everybody else, and our attitudes, our outlook, the way we look at things, the way we think, has all been conditioned by this state of dishonesty, where at all costs we must avoid really facing the facts. We will choose the facts that we look at, to support some theory that we evolved, to make us feel better, to make us feel less guilty, less ashamed, to obscure the fears that are present and continually exerting an influence. What confusion! What irrationality is the real state of human beings on earth, an endeavor to pride oneself on being rational and intelligent but really being thoroughly controlled by this irrational state, thoroughly controlled by superstition.

Human beings pride themselves in these days that they are no longer superstitious like their ancestors were. That's a lie. The superstitions these days are much more sophisticated – that's the only

difference – and we are able to convince ourselves that we are rational
beings. It is not true at all as long as these subconscious controls
operate in human experience. It is these things that cause people to
behave the way they do, and it doesn't take very much to observe the
irrational behavior of human beings. And if one is honest, it doesn't
take very much to observe one's own irrational behavior. How many
times have you said, 'Well, I don't know why I did that'? People
always are trying to rationalize so that they may do what they want to
do and feel justified in doing it. Sometimes, of course, it gets down
to a more or less blatant point, where the individual says, 'Oh, well, to
hell with it. I'm going to do what I want to do anyway.' But what
human beings want to do is based in this totally irrational stuff in the
subconscious levels of the human mind, and it leads to nothing. It is
the state of the dying soul, the soul that is moving toward the experience of nothing.

All this sort of thing must be faced, in a general sense to start with
perhaps, because if we try too quickly to face it individually speaking
we discover that it is virtually impossible to do. It's too terrible to
look into the mirror of self-revealment and to discover the awful state
in which we actually are. However, back of that awful state is something that is real, something that is true, the potential of the living
soul; but we can't get to what is back there without facing and meet-
ing what is in between. We can't forever be running away, at least not
without landing up in oblivion, oblivion for the human race just as
surely as it has been for the individuals who compose the human race.

Spontaneous creation is unacceptable to human beings, except in
the realm of religious fancy perhaps, because of all these subconscious
things; not because it is actually incomprehensible but because it is
unacceptable, because if it is accepted it immediately requires that
we face our own failure and that we see that that failure has been
entirely unnecessary. We can't blame anyone else. We can't blame
our heredity, because we would not exist at all if the potential of the
living soul weren't present; and that potential centers in what was
called the Lord God, what we have recently referred to as the irresistible force, the irresistible force which we know in one of its primary aspects as the experience of life itself, the experience of being
alive, even though not adequately so. The spontaneous creation, as

has been indicated, is not something which happened instantaneously, because, as we have recognized, in this world, this dimensional world of time and space, there is nothing instantaneous. The most instantaneous thing is light perhaps, but even that travels at 186,000 miles a second. It isn't instantaneous. In the world which we know, there is nothing instantaneous. The creation of man was not instantaneous; it occupied a cycle of time. Man was formed of the dust of the ground. Even when it is put this way, it indicates a cycle of time, a sequence. And the Lord God breathed into the nostrils of His creation the breath of life, His creation having been formed, and we have seen how this happens in the present experience, how at the point where the babe is born breathing starts. There was no breathing before that except on the part of the mother, and yet things were taken care of all right in spite of that fact.

So there is an unfoldment, a creative process, and this is true of the spontaneous creation of man. If there is spontaneous combustion, for instance, that certainly is not an instantaneous thing. It gets hotter and hotter and hotter until it combusts – whatever it is, the haystack or whatever. There is a cycle, there is a movement, there is a period of time involved. And so in the creation of man. Man is now created and so it doesn't need to be done again. It's no use looking around and saying, 'Well, I would like to observe how it's done.' It's done. We can observe in principle how it's done, however, by recognizing what happens in relationship to the forming of our own physical bodies, a process which occupies approximately twenty-one years. Just a moment in the cycles of eternity, a spontaneous creation. Individually we have had the experience, physically speaking, of spontaneous creation. Why should it be so strange then? It happens millions of times every year. It's taken for granted now. But the human mind gets all twisted around when it begins to try to think of it in terms of what may have been originally, because it can't see what may have been originally, by reason of all this stuff which is in between. There is no means of penetrating that stuff without facing it. If you need to move through a fog, you will never move through the fog without proceeding into it. You may turn your back on it and say, 'It isn't there,' but it is. It doesn't make any difference to the fog, does it? And the only way you can come through it is to turn and face it. And there is very much to be faced by human beings, that the truth may finally be seen and known for what it is. As long as this distorted, colored state of consciousness exists, human beings by no means can know the truth. It's impossible. All their searching produces only what is seen through the colored and distorted spectacles of their own sub-conscious state. As long as that subconscious state is a mess, which it is, what they see is a mess.

'Blessed are the pure in heart: for they shall see God,' for they shall see the truth, because all this stuff has been cleared out. Well, that looks like a colossal task, doesn't it? What are you going to do? Get mental shovels of some kind and clean the barn? Do you think human beings as they now know themselves could do it? Of course not. The living soul was created by the Lord God. If the living soul is to be re-created, it must also be by the Lord God, because there is a willing-ness to let it occur and there is a willingness to move in the re-creative cycles in whatever way may be necessary. And part of that necessity is to face facts, to begin to be honest. Even though the dishonesty may have been inadvertent, it was still dishonesty, and they say that igno-rance of the law is no excuse. Now we begin to become increasingly cognizant of the law, so there is that much less excuse, that we may face facts in the process, the creative process, the re-creative process, by which man is formed once again, not only out of the dust of the ground – that has already been done – but from the standpoint of the true breath of life which causes this activated dust of the human body to be a living soul. And that job is not done by the human intellect. It is done by the Lord God, whoever the Lord God is. It is done on a basis which the human intellect does not comprehend. After all, the human intellect wasn't on hand to start with to get the job done. It was done very successfully, I suspect chiefly because the self-centered human intellect of man wasn't on hand to disrupt things. And it will be done in exactly the same way now, to the extent that that usurper gets out of the driver's seat and allows it to happen. There's no problem. The yoke is easy, the burden is light, but the job is done by the Lord God.

And so we are here to let that job be done, not merely in expec-tation that it's going to be done for the world, for everybody else in other words, but it is going to be done for oneself. Responsibility is taken again for oneself, to offer oneself, or what one has known of oneself, to the working of this creative process, in the absolute assurance that what one has known of oneself is not what one really is. The experience of what one really is is yet to come by reason of spontaneous creation. Before man was created, man wasn't. The same condition prevails now. Man isn't. There's a strange creature here who dishonestly claims to be man, but man isn't present, so we have the right condition. Let the spontaneous creation of man occur. And by the way, when we let it occur, we then know how it occurs. There's no mystery anymore. And we don't have to try to generate some theory as to how man happens to be around. He isn't around; that's the truth of the matter.

And so let us permit man to be formed out of the dust of the ground, with the breath of life breathed into his nostrils so that he is once again a living soul.

The Wheel

We have come to the sixth month of the year of our Lord 1973; this is the third day, the time of our Sunday morning service. In about another six months another member of the family of our solar system will be visiting the core of that system: a comet will be passing in the vicinity of the sun at that time. This should be a rather spectacular event. This particular comet is supposed to be about fifty times more brilliant than Halley's comet, which is recorded as having been rather remarkable on its last circuit around the sun. The tail of this comet is supposed to extend over about one sixth of the sky.

Comets, in times past, have usually been looked upon as being portents of some kind, and that's right, of course. A body of this nature could not make a close approach into the core of the solar system without having an influence. There are more or less obvious physical influences evident, but there is, of course, more than that. One could say that insofar as human experience is concerned there are undoubtedly psychological influences. Human beings may view with alarm or with composure what occurs. Very often such events are looked upon as more or less mechanical; in fact, it wasn't so long ago that the universe was considered to be a mechanical operation. However, the fact is, of course, that the universe is a living organism and, while it operates according to the rules and regulations of that organism, it is no less alive than your own physical body, which, incidentally, also operates according to the rules and regulations of the organism. But one would hardly look upon a living human body merely as a mechanical contrivance; neither is the universe, nor indeed the solar system itself, or, if we wish to bring it closer to home, this very planet upon which we exist. Life is inherent throughout;

some of the rules and regulations are recognized by human beings but this in no sense denies the fact of life.

So the approach of this comet is not merely a mechanical thing but has effect at many levels, from the physical through the psychological to the spiritual. I wish to emphasize the fact that it is a living experience. Of course, the comet has already been spotted by somebody and the calculations are being made according to the rules and regulations that seem to govern the movement of a comet. Here is a visitor, part of our family, who no doubt should be welcomed into the midst for a brief sojourn before departing for other parts.

Nothing occurs that is not related to everything. This is true, of course, on this rather larger scale. Obviously, even from the physical standpoint, various influences are exerted upon the planets of this solar system by the comet and upon the comet by the planets, also upon the sun and by the sun. This is true also on the smaller scale of our individual lives: we have an influence on each other for good or ill, as the case may be, and this will be determined by the nature of our own movement. Depending upon whether it is aligned with the rules and regulations which govern it or whether we are attempting to move in a direction which has been decided upon by the self-centered approach, our influence will be either constructive or destructive. Most people give very little consideration to what the rules and regulations might be. They seem to be so nebulous in human consciousness that it has become necessary to devise a whole host of rules and regulations humanly established: we have law books full of them. Actually, all this is quite unnecessary if all concerned were interested in moving with the rules and regulations that actually govern. These are not written in books but they certainly are very real. We know a little about some of these rules and regulations. What has been called the law of gravity comes into the picture here, of course, and we do take it into account or suffer the consequences. This is not the only law which relates to our experience. Most of these laws – in fact, all of them – are just as seemingly intangible as gravity. You certainly can't somehow isolate gravity and get hold of it, put it in a bottle! Neither can you isolate and get hold of the rules and regulations which govern human conduct, so that they may be examined under a microscope. Just because they are seemingly intangible and invisible doesn't deny their existence, as anyone who has fallen down the stairs can testify.

So there is much that is not easily perceptible – or perceptible at all, as far as that is concerned – by the physical senses. The results of its presence are known by reason of the physical senses; but there is this realm of law and order presently operative, eternally operative, throughout the whole universe, and we are included within that scope. It relates very specifically to human function, but I have never seen any evidence of a course on this subject in our educational systems. It seems rather a sad neglect. Of course, perhaps the reason why there has been no course has been because there hasn't been anyone to teach it; human beings haven't known. Occasionally they find little bits and pieces and put together a course on psychology, for instance, which doesn't really achieve very much. It is the realm that is occupied by what is called psychology that either connects the external physical experience of a person with the reality of spirit or divides. The self-centered psychological state has been a divisive influence, so that, to an increasing degree over the years, the individual finds that his physical experience is being separated from spirit, until the final moment comes when the separation is complete; but, equally, this psychological area could be the means of connection, of maintaining and increasing the connection between the core of spirit and the periphery of physical form and experience. But the self-centered consciousness has tended to divide because of the self-centered nature.

These things can be illustrated in various ways but a very elementary illustration may be provided by a wheel. This which I hold is actually a 7″ reel for recording tape, but it is a wheel; it has a rim and center point. Now, the rim of the wheel may be used to illustrate the environment, the individual environment. You as a person are in that environment, so your position is somewhere on the rim of the wheel, at the closest point presumably. Life operates through the environment. We could say that here is the wheel of life. The movement is through the environment; in other words, the wheel turns. Your position in relationship to that environment is always at the closest point to where you are, so you stay put but the wheel turns.

Now, there is a natural movement to that wheel; it naturally turns according to the rules and regulations which govern its turning; they are a reality whether anyone knows about it or not. Insofar as we individually are concerned, it behooves us to find out what those rules and regulations are. If we try to live without regard to them it will be no wonder if we find ourselves in trouble most of the time, and the trouble deepens as the years go by. Having been born into this self-centered state, we find ourselves, initially, self-centered people. As has been emphasized before, self-centeredness in the true design, according to the rules and regulations of life, is right and proper in the initial stages of human unfoldment; in other words, a child is self-centered. However, we are not supposed to remain children all our lives. The distinction between a true adult and a child relates to this matter of self-centeredness: a child is self-centered; a true adult is not. In other words there has been an emergence out of that self-centered condition. As we have noted, in present human experience that emergence apparently never comes and, regardless of age, human beings tend to remain self-centered or childish.

Now, using this illustration of the wheel, we will say that the natural movement of the wheel is – if you are looking down upon it, with the wheel horizontal – clockwise. It moves around in this fashion. We look out into the environment and we observe what is there, interpreting it, of course, according to the nature of what is in our own consciousness. In self-centeredness we never see things as they really are – never – because we are bound to see things through our self-centered consciousness; we have no other way of seeing things as long as we remain self-centered. But we see what we think we see, and looking at this imagination we tend to decide, on the basis of our self-centeredness, what we want and what we don't want. Of course, this is all a fantasy, because we don't really see anything as it is and we don't know actually what it is that we should rightly receive or what it is that should rightly move away from us. The movement of life, the wheel of life, the rim of the wheel of life, through the environment takes care of this if we will let it, but it cannot do so as long as we remain self-centered.

This is why a child needs parents and others to provide some sort of guidance and control. It's too bad, isn't it, if the child remains a child psychologically speaking but grows up physically speaking, so that you still have a child in an adult body. Of course, a child in an adult body is inclined to assume that because there is an adult body present the childish state has been left behind, but that isn't the fact of the matter if self-centeredness still prevails. So the child tries to act like an adult, and there is nothing more grotesque than a child acting as an adult. It may be kind of cute if the child is still a child physically speaking: 'Well, isn't that cute!' But it isn't cute when an adult body is there; it becomes a very dangerous thing, because the child has no faintest idea of what he is doing. He is governed by externals, by the environment, and by his or her reaction to that environment. Where there is self-centeredness there are the governing factors of fear and greed. These are the two wants: the individual wants some things to come closer and he also wants to get away from some things.

So, standing on the rim of the wheel, here, he looks out into the environment and sees something on the rim a little further away that on the basis of his childish view is desirable. He sees it there and tends to reach out to it and try to pull it toward him. Of course, this reverses the movement of the wheel if he succeeds – and it is possible to succeed in relationship to oneself. You can't stop the wheel moving in its true direction insofar as the overall picture is concerned, but in one's own personal experience one may. So you find something out here, some one or some thing, some circumstance, that seems to be pleasing, and the endeavor is to pull this thing in; but you will note that the wheel is just one wheel and if you pull it in on this side, it is going out on the other side; so, in pulling this in, it is taking something else away.

Where there is an endeavor to get something, it is accompanied by the experience of losing something – always. That's the rule; that's the regulation. You can't buck the system and get away with it; this is the way it works. Human beings function on this basis, of course. Then, on the other hand, they see something else that they don't like, that they don't want, and they try to push it away, to get rid of it; but lo and behold, here it comes around this side! 'That which I feared has come upon me!' So it is.

Human beings in their living ignore what is illustrated by this nice little reel here and then wonder why troubles of all kinds ensue. They go blithely on their way, ignoring the rules and regulations, and the cop comes along, of course, and taps them on the shoulder. This is the way it works. In the human sense some people imagine that they can get away with breaking the law, and they do sometimes, but, from the standpoint of the law of life, you can't get away with it; it's impossible. It really doesn't require a police force to enforce the law; it's self-enforcing. If we do ignore it, well, we land up in jail, increasingly confined. This is human experience, considered to be more or less normal in this self-centered state. I suppose one could say it is normal in the self-centered state.

So, obviously, the approach to one's experience in living should not be based in this matter of wanting or trying to get anything. The wheel is moving anyway, on the basis of its true nature, the true nature of life moving through you. Something rightly is moving out from you; you do exert an influence. The influence is creative when it is the influence of the true nature of life moving from you. The influence is destructive if you are endeavoring to frustrate the true movement of life by your own self-centered wants and desires, by trying to get what you think you want or get rid of what you think you don't want. In either case there is interference with the true movement of life. Interference with the true movement of life causes what should be the connecting link in you to become the dividing link in you, so that there is increasing division between the source of your own life and your external experience; the cleavage becomes greater. The concern, then, should be to discover how to allow the connection to be rightly made and maintained.

There is no need to be afraid that anything is going to be lost, because the wheel works, and while something moves out from you around one side of the wheel, at the same time something is moving to you around the other side. If what is moving from you is right, what is moving to you will be right; and this is the basis of right fulfilment in experience in living. It can't be gotten, because in trying to get it there is an endeavor to interfere with the right movement of this wheel. Here is a rule and a regulation which is operative in everyone. How foolish, then, to ignore it.

Children ignore it because they don't know any better and they are self-centered. The result of ignoring it is the experience of self-centeredness. Children are very much intent on trying to get what they think they want, because the capacity is not yet developed to the point where they could allow to be given into living expression what is true to life. Of course, in a child this is done more or less automatically in the subsurface levels of consciousness, but the child has not yet learned to permit the right control to be operative from within himself; so the control has to be extended externally for the time being, until the capacity is developed. Unfortunately, in this self-centered world, it is never developed adequately to allow spirit to control; the environment continues to control and the individual is governed by what he thinks about the environment. Whether he approves of it or disapproves of it, it governs him.

So, obviously, the need in true education which allows a person to mature is to discover what it is that life is giving through you, so that you may align yourself with that giving. When you do this, then you are not contending with life; you are not psychologically a divisive force but are providing a connection between the movement of life and the physical form through which it is moving, so that there then begins to be one thing. Heaven and earth are known to be one, spirit and form are one, because the psychological connection is made. Now the psychological connection is made to the extent that self-centeredness is relinquished, so that there is a willingness to observe and to participate in what it is that life would give through you, what it is that is fitting to find expression through your capacities in living in relationship to whatever the circumstance in the environment may be. No longer are you looking at the circumstance and approving of it or disapproving of it. You accept the circumstance for whatever it is and discover what it is that you should express, in alignment with life, into that circumstance; not for the objective of getting something for yourself, not for the objective of getting rid of something from yourself, but simply to let life move in its true nature. If you are concerned with this in the giving aspect, the receiving aspect will take care of itself. Here it comes around the other side, and because it is right giving on one side it will be right receiving on the other: no judgment involved, no attitude taken 'Well, this is what I want' or 'This is not what I want.' That is the childish state; that is the self-centered state, maintained by human beings generation after generation for millennia and producing hell on earth in various ways, until we have reached the point of this final climactic hell which is here, and yet to come. The question is as to whether we are going to do what we may to intensify the hell, by our wants and trying to get, or whether we are going to permit the experience of the heaven because we are moving with the heaven.

We are primarily and properly concerned – always, in relationship to all things, everything – with what it is that life would give, the life specifically moving through oneself. What would it give into this situation that is right and fitting and needful in the particular situation? With such an attitude there is no need to judge the situation. Let it be what it is, but be very sure that what moves through you into that situation is what should be moving through you into that situation. And if it is that, it will not be the result of your reaction to the situation, it will not be based in your desires, your wants, as they relate to the circumstance – to the circumstance, the thing, the person. You live from the core of your own being and you are psychologically concerned that that core should find expression and release. In doing so, of course, you come to know yourself, you come to know what you are, what life is in you.

Now this is the way, at a different level, in which what is called 'nature' functions. As our Master pointed out, the flowers don't have to give thought to what is coming to them, what is to be received, because it is automatic. If they are true to themselves, if the bird is true to itself in the expression of its birdliness, then what is required to sustain the bird comes to the bird. Of course, these cycles have been considerably disrupted by reason of self-centered human function, because human beings have an influence. Whether they realize it or not, whether they know what that influence is or not, they have an influence – not only upon other human beings, not only upon their circumstances, but upon everything throughout the whole of nature and beyond. We come out of childishness when we begin to take responsibility for the rightness of our own expression relative to the environment that is present with us, when our first flush of feeling is in this regard rather than 'Is this going to be pleasing to me? Is this going to make me happy? Am I going to enjoy this?' Isn't that the usual first flush of human feeling? Having this sort of an attitude the individual then proceeds to try to manipulate what it is that he is aware of in his environment. Because it is pleasing, he tries to get it; if it is displeasing, he tries to push it away. If he tries to get it, then without realizing it he is losing something at the same time; and if he tries to push the ill thing away, well, it comes right around to him on the other side. So, by trying to get, the person loses what he tries to get; and by trying to get rid of, the person gains what he tries to get rid of. And life sure becomes a battle; it seems so essential to be struggling.

Whereas the simple expedient of recognizing that life is moving rightly through you now would allow you in your intelligence to associate yourself with that movement, so that what was expressed was expressed on the basis of a concern for its rightness and fittingness with respect to the particular circumstance which is the opportunity for the movement of life. Lo and behold, the blessings come in the cycle of life more or less unobserved, not observed until they come right up against you, because you are not looking for them. But suddenly there they are! And what comes on this basis is so much more marvelous than anything that could be dragged to you on the other that there is no comparison whatsoever. Yet how foolishly human beings insist upon sitting in their self-centeredness and trying to get what they think they want. How often have you tried to get something on this basis and found that when and if you got it, it wasn't what you expected at all, because you didn't really see what it was you were trying to get? In self-centeredness you can't. Life sees; life knows what should be. And you may share that seeing and knowing with life, but not all on your little self-centered own.

Agree with life, agree quickly, and let whatever it is that is moving through you of life in the moment be freely given because you are no longer concerned with any getting. As should be obvious, this does not mean that there is no receiving; it means that you are simply not concerned with getting. The receiving comes automatically when the giving is right, and what you receive will be what you should receive to permit the greater fulfilment of your giving. So the cycle of life intensifies and the movement is found to be a joy forever, because it is a thing of beauty – an eternal joy, because life is eternal. If you ignore the movement of life and try to frustrate it by your own self-centeredness, you lose life and life is not eternal insofar as your own experience is concerned. But the fact of the matter is, the truth is, that life is eternal. So how about being with it? – being with life, offering what is right and what is fitting into the circumstance of the moment without judgment, that life through you may freely move, bringing on the returning cycle what is fitting and right for you. Is this not a description of fulfilment?

In our meditation we have been considering a more or less elementary rule of life; untaught, as far as I know, in the educational system, but first grade, very elementary. Yet unless we learn what is in first grade, how are we going to learn anything else? Some young people have difficulty in the later grades of education because they never learned to read – or write, for that matter. They never learned what should come in the early grades, and it is a handicap, isn't it? Let us put first things first and learn through experience, so that we know. When we know this, we are in position to know what comes next and next and next, so that we may emerge through the divine educational system with our degree, the degree which enables us to live – the degree of life, something that is very practical and very useful.

The Art and Science of Living

It is remarkable how little consideration is given to the art and science of living, in the world as we know it. Much is considered in the curriculum of the high school and in university but, at least in the public sector of things, no interest seems to be displayed in the art and science of living; no courses. But, whether this subject is taught or not, we find ourselves under the necessity of remaining alive for a few years. Why is there such a lack of interest in this particular area? Principally, I suppose, because there are so few qualified teachers, and also because perchance it might interfere with what people want to do with themselves. It might be discovered, for instance, that there are very definite rules and regulations if life is to be experienced; and human beings are not too happy about such things; they want to have what they call freedom, freedom to do as they please. This is permissible while life remains, but if this so-called freedom is exercised life doesn't remain very long, because there are these rules and regulations. Should they be ignored, then disease, death and disaster ensue.

We ourselves have, presumably, acknowledged the truth of this, but the question is as to how much real interest has been displayed, both in gaining a deeper understanding of the art and science of living and also a deeper experience of it. As I have indicated, all too many people endeavor to avoid any consideration in this regard, in case it might interfere with the way they want to conduct their own affairs. Undoubtedly it would interfere, but how foolish to follow the path which inevitably leads into trouble rather than to turn attention toward a discovery of what life is really all about.

Presumably we spend an hour or two a week investigating this area, and we are examined and graded twenty-four hours a day the rest of the week. Now, whether a person studies the subject or not, he is still examined and graded during the hours of his weekly experience. In high school or university it is recognized that there must be a way of determining whether a person has learned anything, and so there are various kinds of examinations, which must be passed if one is to continue to experience the greater education. But in the area of life's examination there is failure, as evidenced by many things, by all the troubles which human beings experience; and because of this human beings have a sense of failure. It may not be clearly recognized as to why it is there or even clearly recognized that it is there, but subconsciously there is this sense of failure, a sense of lack, a sense of inadequacy. Of course, this is uncomfortable, so various methods are used to try to dispose of it.

All this confused state of affairs in human experience is, as we well know, consequent upon the fact that man, male and female, has become separated from the universal whole. Human beings individually feel themselves to be isolated, but the fact of the matter is that the whole of mankind is isolated. It has isolated itself from participation in the overall operation of the universal whole. Some say this is a separation from God – that may be one way of describing the situation – but it is a fact. Human beings, for the most part, have little awareness that they really are a part of even this little whole here on the surface of this planet. Man has been acting as though he was separate and apart from what is usually called nature; he can stand in his exalted position, apparently – according to his own view at least – and observe nature, as though he himself wasn't a part of nature. Because of this false positioning he sees everything in a very distorted fashion, and apparently his central interest relates to how he may live with himself – that is, human beings may live with each other – set up some sort of a society and all the relationships that are in that society, so as to make man content. Here is obvious isolation: mankind completely encased in plastic and separate from the rest of the universe. Of course, he finds now particularly that he has to take into account some of nature because it is necessary to his continued existence; but if he could dispense with nature on the surface of this planet and continue to exist and to be in a condition of satisfactory relationship within the body of mankind, he would do it! In other words, there is no awareness of the fact that he is a part of anything more than mankind; whereas a little common sense immediately indicates that mankind couldn't exist at all if it wasn't for the fact that there is a planet to exist on and, therefore, the fact of the planet is an important point. And the planet would not be a suitable habitation for man if it was not in correct relationship with the sun at least; so immediately there is an obvious connection between man and the solar system. He is not quite so sure as to what the connection might be between the solar system and the galaxy, but obviously the solar system is a part of the galaxy.

In any case, man has this isolationist viewpoint and, individually speaking, we also find ourselves in isolation – all because of the failure to pass the examination and to reach the necessary grades in the art and science of living. So, individually speaking, we feel somewhat alone, isolated, lonely. Now this sense of isolation is an indication of the fact that there is a need to be restored to proper relationship to the universal whole. This is what this individual human loneliness means, but this is not the way that human beings interpret it. Because a person feels lonely and isolated he looks around for something or someone to fill the void; and if in this attitude he is successful in discovering someone who more or less satisfactorily for the moment seems to fill that void, he has thereby defeated his own movement toward maturity or the true experience of living.

Human beings are mutually parasitic in this sense. The person feels the emptiness inside himself. 'How is it going to be filled?' he says. 'Well, I must have a friend,' he says. So he looks around to find someone who will more or less fill the requirement of this void. But if he preys upon somebody else in this fashion – and, presumably, if there is a mutual affinity here the other person is preying upon the first person – all movement toward the experience of the art and science of living ceases. The individual cannot mature, because the only way by which maturity comes and one may become aware of the truth of oneself is by letting it fill the void from within oneself. In other words, there is no one who can permit the void in you to be filled except you, and if you try to get someone else to do it you prevent yourself from experiencing what it would mean to let that void be filled. This emptiness in you can only be filled by you, not by anybody else.

If interest is turned toward the art and science of living, this is one of the first things that become apparent. Those who are trying to fill the voids in themselves by using other people – and it's not always other people; it's things too – to try to fill themselves up in this regard so that this gnawing loneliness is taken away, completely frustrate what is essential in the experience of living and they become addicted to whatever it is they think is necessary to fill the void in themselves. So a person imagines that if whatever it is he has chosen to fill the void in himself were taken away it would be a terrible thing; it would be disaster; he couldn't live anymore. Sometimes in the field of what is called love, this idea is very strong. People say, 'I couldn't live without so-and-so!' The point is that the person can't live with so-and-so, actually, because it is completely frustrating the experience of the art and science of living.

This seems totally contradictory to the human consciousness be-cause, after all, we have to get along together; we have to have relationships; we have to have friends. Oh, yes, that's true, but on what basis? If it is based in the fact that one is lonely and therefore is trying to fill one's void of loneliness by using other people and other things, one must remain in a very childish state, never experiencing what it means to live, never experiencing the truth of oneself. It is impossible on that basis, because one has blocked the very thing that should be the connecting point with the truth of life itself. If you assuage your loneliness on this basis you destroy yourself. Yet this is what everybody is trying to do – a complete violation of the rules and regulations of life. If you violate the rules and regulations of life you stop living! Now, it is a more or less gradual process and people don't realize what is happening. Some do wake up somewhere along the way and say to themselves, 'What on earth have I been doing?' Well, then, they may have some little interest in the art and science of living and can begin to find out how it works.

Presumably in other fields of education people are interested in finding out how various things work, but life . . . ! Yet how quickly people establish habit patterns and addictions early in life, out of which they find it virtually impossible to come later on. There is a problem of drug addiction and alcohol addiction in the world; these are the main areas that are considered to be addiction. But there is addiction in every direction. Almost everything that human beings do is based in their addictions. They are controlled by these addictions. 'Oh, I couldn't live without this and without that and without the other person.' That's an addiction, obviously, because the fact of the matter is that until first things are put first the person cannot live. Emphasis has been placed on what has been called the first great commandment because this refers to what is first necessary. When what is first necessary is considered as being first, then everything else can fall into place, because the individual will not be looking around anymore to assuage his own sense of isolation and loneliness.

There isn't a human being on the face of the earth who does not have this sense of isolation and loneliness, and because of this which is present he tries desperately to fill it up. How few people will pay any attention to the true way of allowing this experience of living to come. They want to fill these things up in their own way, according to their own ideas of what they think they want, of what they think is necessary. If it seems as though anyone succeeds in this field it is a fatal success; it kills the person. It kills all those who indulge in this addiction, just as is true of the particular areas upon which attention is focused these days. 'Oh, we have a terrible problem of drug addiction; and now alcohol ...!' Yes, it's a problem all right, but it is not a different problem from the problem of all human experience. It's all addiction. There is this endeavor to fasten like a parasite on somebody else, to suck somebody else's life, in order to fill one's own sense of void, one's own sense of loneliness. That is selfish self-centeredness. This is glorified in various ways as being the natural thing for man, very romantic at times and so on, but it is all hogwash; it is all an endeavor to avoid the necessity of being honest and coming again to the point of recognition as to the source of the filling of the void of loneliness in oneself. It cannot be filled, rightly, through anyone beyond oneself.

When you begin to let it be filled in the right way from within yourself, then you are not being impelled into relationships with people in order to satisfy yourself; in other words, it is not a self-centered thing. It begins to be a mature thing because there is consideration as to the value of any particular relationship in the fulfilling of the purposes of life, not the individual idea of purpose that may be in the person but the actual purposes of life. Life has a purpose; you wouldn't exist if it wasn't so. It produced you ... for what purpose? So that you could say, 'Oh goody, I have life; now I can use it for my purposes'? But life produced you, and if you don't allow life to continue to produce its purposes for you because of you, you isolate yourself from life and you are very lonely. And then, 'Oh, how can I assuage this terrible gnawing loneliness within me? I must find somebody to do this,' and various relationships develop on this basis, and we have a childish condition everywhere in the world, a condition of childish addiction. We have children playing with their toys: 'Now it's bedtime, you have got to let go of your toy.' Waah! That's the way it is, isn't it, with children. Children become addicted to their toys. That may be all right up to a point with children, but gradually they need to learn to let go of them, because even with children the teddy bear, or whatever it is, is used to fill the void in the childish heart, but it can't be filled that way. It is more or less obvious that one can't spend the rest of one's life with a teddy bear, or even a blanket! So usually the addictions change; the teddy bear is dropped and something else is taken up. But it is still an addiction. It is always an addiction if it relates to some external thing with respect to which the individual would feel utterly desolate if it was taken away.

Is there anything that can be taken away from you that would cause you to feel desolate? I am sure the answer is in the affirmative. If that is so, then whatever it is is in some measure at least being used by you to cover up your sense of aloneness. It indicates some area in you in which you are immature, some area which you have not allowed to be filled with what you are, the truth of yourself, so that your heart might be filled with the expression of love – not trying to get love from anybody, not expecting love from anybody, but your expression of love – and your mind filled with the truth, the right control and understanding of design as to the manner in which that love is properly expressed; and your body filled with life, life which reveals itself in health. The addictions pass away when you are taking the responsibility for this, for letting your heart be filled with love, not from somebody else but from within yourself, so that what you do, the way you act, everything that finds expression through you, will be an enfoldment, a blessing, an understanding of the needs of others, to inspire others to let it be so with themselves, so that they may participate in this for themselves. It is the inspiration offered through true education which brings maturity in anyone. You may, by your expression of the truth of love in living, reveal the way, the truth and the life. That is what is meant by the way, the truth and the life.

There it is, and you do not feel lonely anymore, because you have an awareness, a consciousness, deep within yourself that you are a part of the universal whole. That awareness may not be adequately in form yet out here in the experience of living; in other words, the relationships that are right on this basis may not yet have taken adequate form. But it isn't that which causes you not to feel lonely. I seem to recall something our Master said when He was on earth, about His disciples forsaking him. He said, 'You will all forsake me and leave me alone in the external sense but not really alone, because the Father is with me; my awareness of relationship to the universal whole is still there regardless of what happens in the external sense; everything can be taken away' – as it was in His experience. Everything was taken away, but it made no difference to Him; He was still Himself.

When we learn to let these voids – which are undoubtedly there, because man has isolated himself from the whole – be filled, then the sense of isolation and aloneness vanishes away and we are in position to function intelligently and with maturity in our relationships with others. They are never based on an addiction. They are never such that we would be completely desolated if they were removed. Now, all human relationships will, sooner or later, be removed, right? So many people in life – or what they call life – go through successive experiences of desolation. Sometimes it becomes so devastating that the individual takes his own life, commits suicide; but whether he does it with a swift stroke of the razor blade or whatever, or whether he dies from natural causes (as it is said!), it is all consequent upon the same thing: a violation of the rules and regulations of life.

Let us find again our burning interest in the art and science of living. Is it too much, do you think, just to have an hour or two a week for this study, in view of the fact that we have at least several decades of living to do? Isn't it a peculiar thing how human beings will go along with education in all kinds of fields, but in the one central field where it is most important they won't have anything to do with it? This, of course, emphasizes the awful self-centeredness which is the overwhelming state of people everywhere. What is the art and science of living? Let us pass our examinations in this regard so that we do not have this inbuilt sense of failure. We are examined. Every human being on the face of the earth is constantly being examined and there is constant evidence of failure, so it is not surprising if people feel that they are failures.

This emptiness, this loneliness, this sense of isolation, is present in each human being. He is trying to live in his little cell, doesn't like it in there alone, wants somebody else to share it with him. This is the way to fatal addiction. It is not the romantic fulfilment that so many people suppose. The romantic fulfilment comes because there is a love of life, a love of what life really is, and when we discover this by living it we find that fulfilment ourselves. Because we know the reality of fulfilment in this way, it is reflected in our external experience. The external fulfilment comes as a result of the internal fulfilment. How often we have said that the world around us is simply a reflection of what we are as human beings. If human beings look for external fulfilment, how would they find it? By manipulating external events? By becoming involved with all these addictions? Of course not, but by experiencing the internal fulfilment. When that is known it is reflected externally. Then it's right; then it's life, not a decreasing experience of existence, where the most vibrant time of experience is in the early years and then the good wine runs out. In the true state of the marriage feast, the good wine is kept to the last – an interesting situation, completely unknown by human beings because they have squandered everything in riotous living; that is, uncontrolled living, uncontrolled by the rules and regulations of life; then life goes!

But here we see the value of the sense of loneliness. It is most valuable because it may, if we will let it, turn our attention to the art and science of living. When it does that, there is the answer. There the emptiness is filled. And it is one's own experience; it is not dependent upon somebody else, and that is success, that is victory. If you have to depend upon somebody else to fill it up, that's failure, utter failure, and maintaining the childish state with the teddy bear. So let us accept the opportunity of participating in the true education.

We will only participate in it if we are interested in it. Nobody learns very much at school if he is not interested in the subject. Some of the subjects in school are pretty dry and uninteresting, but unless one generates some sort of interest there is going to be failure. One can generate an interest in anything, but why should it be so difficult to generate an interest in living, rather than in dying? Human interest is almost entirely centered in the processes of dying, in doing the things which bring disease, death and disaster – the three d's. So, living is available to anyone. How much interest is there really? or how much addiction? All addictions are dissolved by coming to know oneself, by reaching the experience of what has been called true identity. Very often people see this and are delighted to see it, but who does anything about it? Very, very few. Why? Because it interferes with the accepted experiences of dying. So I draw your attention to the true education in the art and science of living. Let there be interest here and we will live.

The Right Answer

I would like to read some verses from the 38th chapter of the Book of
Job this morning. It is said of Job that he was a perfect and an upright
man, 'one that feared God, and eschewed evil'. The human interpretation of these words might picture Job as a good, religious man,
rather austere and straitlaced. This would not be the truth of the
matter. How often human beings interpret something and then reject
their interpretation, never having seen the truth at all. In fact, this is
done continuously, because it is a long, long time since anyone knew
the truth. Of course, sometimes the interpretation is pleasing, in
which case the individual may accept it. But all this relates to a realm
of imagination, evil imagination, a realm of vanity and foolishness,
the realm where human beings presently exist.

A few people have come, or begun at least, to recognize the state of
affairs in human experience and have turned the face of their response toward the truth, that in season they might know it. The Book
of Job itself presents a picture of the pattern of human function, the
meaningless state, until finally Job comes again to the truth. There
was an interim period when the truth was thoroughly obscured from
his conscious awareness. Enlightenment certainly did not come
through the wordiness of his three friends, but eventually, because he
had kept his integrity, the truth emerged in his own consciousness,
from whence alone the truth comes. It does not come from externals;
it does not come from an examination of the environment, even
though we may reach into the furthest distances of space or into the
realm peopled by what are now called atoms. The truth comes from
God, because God is the truth. No one can know the truth while
ignoring God; the terms are synonymous, even though, it may be
recognized, God is more than the truth. The truth is an aspect of the

nature of God. To know the truth, whether we like it or not or whether we believe it or not, we must come to God. The word *God* is another word subject to human interpretation. The interpretations of this word have caused human beings either to accept God, believe in God, or to reject God – but the God is the God of interpretation, not the reality. The reality is only known when we know the truth, yet we cannot know the truth without coming to God.

We cannot come to God if we do not keep our integrity. The very fact that we do keep our integrity is the evidence that the face of our response is turned to God, regardless of the acceptance or rejection of our interpretations. As we have noted many times, it is always the fact that counts, not what the individual imagines. We have had many vain imaginations, but the fact counts. Job kept his integrity. He did not impute anything wrong to God. He did not imagine that with his puny human mind he could determine whether God existed and, if He did, exactly what God was. He was willing to keep his integrity as a man. Here is the secret, if we may call it such – it needn't remain a secret – of the return of a human being to God, so that he may once more know the truth.

The story as it is outlined in the Book of Job relates to all human beings, providing a portrayal of what happens when a person does keep his integrity. Even though the experience may be a difficult one, a painful one, even a tragic one, keeping one's integrity brings a person back to God. It is at the point described in the 38th chapter that this becomes apparent.

'Then the Lord answered Job out of the whirlwind, and said,

'Who is this that darkeneth counsel by words without knowledge?

'Gird up now thy loins like a man; for I will demand of thee, and answer thou me.'

Things are beginning to come back into place evidently, according to this statement. Human beings are accustomed to asking questions. They are accustomed to taking an attitude which tries to get answers. But here we have a reversal of the stance. As long as man casts himself in the role of the one who has a right to demand, he is maintaining a false state. Is this not one of the most outstanding characteristics of human beings these days? They are always making demands. Any courtesy or politeness has gone out of the picture altogether. What human beings think they want seems always nowadays to be couched in terms of demand. This is done quite openly, and yet it is an indication of the lack of integrity in human beings. The truth is that human beings have no right whatsoever to make any demands at all, and yet demands are made on the basis of what are supposed to be human rights.

The question is, in fact, being put to human beings, that human beings may give their answer. One of the answers, apparently, that human beings give is to take the position that they have a right to demand. An outstanding characteristic of Job was that he made no demands; he just kept his integrity. He trusted God, seeing no occasion to make any demands. Is this not the evidence of trust in God? A person who does not trust God feels that it is incumbent upon him to try to get the answer, to make demands. Here is clear evidence of a lack of trust in God. Where there is no trust in God there is no integrity.

The evidence of Job's integrity came as he once more became aware of his true position. This is described as the Lord speaking to Job out of the whirlwind; in other words, Job recognizing that the question was being put to him: 'Answer thou me.' This is the fact with respect to every human being on the face of the earth. The question is being put to you. If you try to twist it around by taking the attitude that you are the questioner, you are in a false position; and if you are in a false position, how could you know the truth? The only way that the truth can be known is to come into the true position, the true position of man, a living soul. In that position, the truth is known; out of that position, the truth is not known and, because it is not known, the constant feeling is of lack and therefore of the necessity of making demands, of trying to get. This very attitude in human beings demonstrates their lack. And, fundamentally, what is that lack? It is the lack of the experience of 'man'. Human beings find themselves in a condition which is in the nature of a void: no experience of the truth of manhood or womanhood. If that were the experience, if manhood and womanhood were known, there would be no necessity to make demands. If demands are made, then here is the evidence of the lack of manhood and womanhood, the lack of integrity.

'Then the Lord answered Job out of the whirlwind, and said,

'Who is this that darkeneth counsel by words without knowledge?

'Gird up now thy loins like a man; for I will demand of thee, and answer thou me.'

This immediately places the human being in his true position, so that he comes out of that state of emptiness where he imagines that he constantly has to make demands, into the position where he may become aware of the question that is being asked of him. Now, of course, this is a portrayal of what happens in human experience when a person keeps his integrity. The Lord speaks out of the whirlwind. Here is something of the spirit of God emerging in the creative cycles into the awareness of the person, so that he finally realizes that the truth is not obtainable, that his needs are not really fillable, from external sources. If he is to experience the truth he must begin answering some questions, not trying to get answers to questions.

Now usually when anyone turns toward God he does so because he is desirous of having his questions answered. It seems a very peculiar thing that in turning to God he should begin to answer questions. The person says, 'Well, how can I answer the questions if God hasn't answered me yet?' But, obviously, the endeavor to get answers from God is still the spirit of self-centeredness, isn't it? where the person continues to insist on the validity of himself, the validity of himself in the false state. 'I want God to answer my questions so that I may feel valid even though in the false state.' All questioning is of this nature, even if it is directed to external things. The god of human beings these days is the god of external things; so it is assumed the answer is going to come from that god, and demands are made upon that god to fill human needs. The god of government, for instance – 'Answer thou me. Fill my needs. Make me secure. Take care of my . . . not my health but my sickness!' The attitude of irresponsibility, the childish attitude which makes demands upon mamma. This is the human state, isn't it? A constant series of demands. 'Fill my needs. Keep me alive. Sustain my false position.' Do you think that the answer really should be provided for this? Of course, ultimately there is no answer for that sort of questioning. As time goes on, the individual finds less and less answer, until there is no answer at all. That was described rather graphically in the story of Elijah and the prophets of Baal, wasn't it? They couldn't, in the end, produce any answer at all. Their demands went unheeded, because they were trying to get God to obey human beings. What utter chaos there would be in the universe if they were to succeed! They never have succeeded, although they are constantly on the verge of succeeding, they think. But what futility!

Human beings are here to answer God, to answer to God, not to demand of God. You can spell the word *God* with a capital *G* or a little *g*; it's all the same thing. Human gods are mostly spelled with a little *g* – idolatry – but it is the attitude itself that is the point. Whether a person makes demands upon what he imagines God with a capital *G* to be or whether he makes demands upon his boss or his wife or his friend or whoever, it is all the same thing, because human beings are here on earth to answer some questions, to make evident the truth. The question is being asked, and the answer is to speak the truth – isn't that right? – to express the truth, to reveal the truth. For instance, the question might be asked, 'Who are you?' That question is being asked constantly, and a great variety of answers are given. As we have been looking at it now, the answer might be, 'I am a demander. I want the answer. I am not interested in giving the answer; I want it.' But who wants it? Obviously, a false person, because the true person is the answer. If you are the answer you give the answer, you don't ask the question. Yet all this seems peculiar in human consciousness because it has become so customary to be a self-centered person and a self-centered person is always making demands.

A child is naturally self-centered and makes demands upon its parents, upon other people. For a child this is quite as it should be; it's part of the process of coming to the point of knowing the truth, rightly. If someone turns toward the Lord, he can only do so as a little child. Only a little child needs to turn to the Lord. This is why one must come as a little child to the Lord. The little child, initially, makes demands, and the needs of the little child are filled one way or another, not so much because the child makes demands as because it is the natural expression of the parents to fill the needs of the child. Sometimes those needs are made more apparent by the demands of the child but sometimes the demands of the child do not really relate to the true need. The parent should be wise enough to give what is needed rather than what the child wants. Now, from the standpoint of someone who turns to the Lord, the Lord provides what is needed, not necessarily what the individual thinks at that point he wants – all the answers to his questions, for instance. That is not the true need.

So, initially, the individual has the attitude of demand because he is coming out of the condition of the false person. The false person demands. The false person is always questioning, always trying to get the answers. One has to start from the place where one is; so this attitude, then, begins to be turned more particularly toward the Lord rather than towards externals. The individual with that attitude is expecting answers, demanding that his needs be filled. 'Give me understanding,' he says, 'so that I can be useful on earth.' 'Heal me,' he says, 'so that I may be able to do what needs to be done on earth.' Very often a person will turn toward the Lord because he is sick; he is demanding health, and he thinks that it is quite all right to do so because, after all, 'God surely wants everybody to be healthy; therefore why shouldn't I demand it?' Because that attitude of demand prevents the experience of health; the attitude of demand prevents the experience of understanding. It is an attitude, here, that we are talking about, the attitude which tries to get answers.

How about accepting an attitude which undertakes to give answers? We are sharing a consideration this morning of these matters. Do you have the feeling that in my speaking I am trying to get an answer? I think you have the sensing that I am giving an answer. If I am in position to give an answer, why are you not in position to give an answer? I do not come in here and sit down in the chair and ask you to tell me what I am to say. Who do you think I ask to tell me what I am to say? Anyone? No, of course not! If I made the demand I would have nothing to say; I would still be looking for the answer. I am interested in giving the answer, to the extent that it may be given in this setting, under this circumstance, on the basis of the pattern of response that is present.

Supposing I came in here with the idea of giving a certain answer. That would mean that I would have to demand a certain setting in order that that answer might be given; so I would be in the position of making demands then, demands on you. You may have the feeling with respect to what is expressed that you have to rise up a little; in other words, that you have to give an answer of some sort. I trust you do feel that way, because that is response. Response is giving the answer, isn't it? If you are in class in school and the teacher asks you a question, your response would be to give the answer. I am giving an answer but at the same time you are giving an answer too. We share this, rightly; this is the basis of our agreement.

In the outline here in this particular chapter in the Book of Job, various questions are asked by the Lord. Do you think He was asking those questions so that He might be edified by the answer that was given? I hardly think so. He was asking the questions first of all to bring to the attention of Job, in this instance, whether he felt capable of answering these questions, and then, taking it a step further, to impress upon Job that he should be able to answer these questions and that if a person is not capable of answering the questions that are asked by the Lord he is not in his right position; he is not yet himself; he does not yet know the truth. If we do not know the truth, what do we know? Presumably something that isn't true. That's a false state, isn't it? It is necessary that we should be convinced, to start with, that we don't know as much as we thought we did. Perhaps this is done more or less gently, because it would be too much of a shock to be told right off the bat that we don't know anything, but the point must be reached – and is reached when we begin to come into true position – where we are willing to acknowledge that we don't know 'nuthin'! Because the person who tries to cling to the idea that he does know something is clinging to his false position. Of course one of the factors here is false pride, isn't it? We don't wish to admit that we are as stupid as we are; because a false person is a stupid person; he's bound to be. Oh, he may be clever, but not yet wise and understanding. That only comes because one is in right position, one is a true person.

To be a true person we must answer these questions, and we answer the specific question that is being put to us as individuals. A question is constantly being put to us as individuals in every moment. It could be said that life examines us to find out what sort of an answer we are going to give. Are we going to give the true answer, or a false one? This is determined by the fact of our own expression in the moment. What are we going to demonstrate? A miserable, weak, foolish human being? A false person? Or are we going to demonstrate integrity, a true person?

Now, the human being, accustomed to demanding answers for everything, thinks that the giving of an answer would simply be to provide an explanation; and the person says, 'Well, I don't really know. I can't give the explanation; I don't know what the answer is.' But that is not the answer. The answer is in what one is in expression, the nature of one's own expression in the moment, the quality of that expression. I suppose in a general sense the question might be couched in these terms: Are you a son or a daughter of God? Now, that question is being asked all the time of every human being on the face of the earth, and almost invariably the wrong answer is given. In effect, the individual says, 'No.' Not in words necessarily, but in the way he or she behaves. What is the quality that finds expression in the individual in the moment? That's the answer that the person is giving to the question that is being asked.

Who are you? Most of those who have called themselves Christians have answered that in words – and in action – 'I am a sinner.' That's not the truth! 'I am' is the name of God, so the person is saying God is a sinner. That is assuming a false position, a false identity, a false state, and in that false state there is the emptiness of the falseness, so the false person imagines, feeling so desperately empty, that he must try to fill that emptiness somehow – hence all the demands. Only an empty person would need to make demands. It is interesting how human beings constantly demonstrate the fact with respect to themselves. No judgment is necessary; just observe the fact. What demands do you make on life? Let us be honest and recognize that life asks us the question, 'Who are you?' If you don't answer correctly, you prove the fact out. If you give anything else but the correct answer, that fact becomes evident. Of course the fact of giving the correct answer becomes evident too. But the evidence of giving the incorrect answer is ultimately death; the evidence of giving the correct answer is presently, and ultimately, life.

'Gird up now thy loins like a man . . . and answer thou me.' Unless a person is interested in giving the right answer, he is not a man. Those who give false answers demonstrate their unmanhood. The question is put; there are two possible answers: aye or nay, I am the truth or I am not. Human beings in every moment of their existence are answering that question one way or the other. That question is being asked more insistently of human beings in these days. This is why the demands of human beings have become so much more insistent; there is a sensing of the question but it is misinterpreted. To the extent that we begin to see what it really is, we are in position to demonstrate the right answer. We cannot demonstrate the right answer if we ourselves are making demands, if we ourselves are trying to get the answer. This places us right back in the condition of childhood, at best. Let us come to the Lord because we are willing to answer Him. Very much consideration has been given to the matter of response, hasn't it? This is what response is – answering, giving the answer. To the extent that we are willing to give the answer, we discover ourselves as the answer and so there is no need to try to get the answer.

The Lord speaks out of the whirlwind – the whirlwind, the spirit moving in the creative cycle – asking for the answer of each one, the answer which is revealed by the person when he demonstrates his integrity and his capacity to move in that creative cycle. The total interest, then, is in answering the question. When the concern is there the truth begins to emerge into expression, and because it is expressed by oneself it is known by oneself. That is the only way the answer may be known on earth. It may be known because human beings, ourselves included, give it. The giving of it is what we call response.

The Spirit of Integrity

People have many opportunities of gathering themselves together for various purposes, for various reasons, but there is only one right reason and this centers in what we may describe by the word *integrity*, a longing to experience the reality indicated by that word. If there are those on earth who are in position to exemplify this spirit of integrity, then there is available a point to which people may come. Only those will come, of course, who have a basic yearning to know the reality of integrity in their own expression of life on earth.

'Come unto me, all ye that labour and are heavy laden, and I will give you rest' from the turmoil, from the conflict, from the distress of human self-centered experience. As long as self-centered attitudes persist, then there is no surcease from human woes. It becomes obvious that there must be a change of viewpoint and attitude from the self-centered approach which is common to human experience if the former things of turmoil, conflict and distress are to pass away. As long as self-centeredness is maintained the results of self-centeredness will be present. There is no human being on the face of the earth who does not have experience of those results. It is quite plain that most people are happy to complain about them – they wouldn't complain so much if they didn't think it made them happy – but there are very few indeed who exhibit any real willingness to come out of the self-centered state.

In order to leave the self-centered state, some other state must be known; there must be movement from one state to another. This other state may well be described by the word *integrity*, the state of integrity, integrity which places primary value in spiritual things rather than in material things. Now, there are lots of people who will nod wisely and say, 'Yes, the world is too materialistic; the values are

78

indeed in the wrong place.' But that's about as far as it goes, because primary values are maintained in material things even though many people object to this state of affairs. There are, therefore, those who fight against the idea of putting value in material things. Because they feel that it is necessary to fight against that state of affairs, they are giving value to it. If there is anything against which you think you have to fight or struggle or contend, obviously you have given value to that thing. And so it is in the world: most of the values that are maintained in the world of human beings are maintained on the basis of fighting against something. There are more 'antis' than any other breed of creature, at least within the scope of the human family. Fighting against what is considered to be wrong or evil certainly gives indication that one gives much weight to what he thinks is wrong or evil.

It is surely far more creative and constructive to give value to what is right, to recognize that true values are spiritual values and to behave as though one recognized that this was the truth. Those who aspire to spiritual experience so often do so on the basis of the fact that they have given so much value to material experience. They think they have to get away from the material experience in order to find the spiritual experience, as though here were two separate things. The spiritual and the material are in fact one. It is because human beings have not seen this to be true that their approach is based in this duality of vision. The idea then becomes that one could not be spiritual without denying the material, or if one accepts the material, then one necessarily denies the spiritual. This is an entirely false view because the fact of the matter is that heaven and earth are one; it is only human beings who are so dumb that they don't know it, and their dumbness is proclaimed by the way they behave. There is a constant battle in one way or another even from the standpoint of those who think of themselves as being peacemakers – they're against war, they're anti war. How about being *for* something so that we give value to what really has value and stop giving value to what hasn't? As we have already noted, it is quite easy to give value to something wrong by being against it. If what is right has value in our experience, then we don't need to fuss about what is wrong and what is wrong is no longer fed our life force to maintain it in existence.

Of course, most people have very little idea as to what is right and what is wrong. This brings us again to the necessity of placing spiritual values in the primary position. If spiritual values are put first, then material things begin to reflect true value and it becomes quite obvious that heaven and earth are one; but if material values are put first because one espouses them or because one fights against them, then spiritual values go by the board and material values have no value either actually. The values which human beings give to material things destroy those concerned, and whether they give those values to material things on the basis of espousing them or fighting against them makes very little difference. Coming again to the state of integrity, where spiritual values are put first, then the real value of everything begins to be comprehended.

To the extent that there begins to be on earth a body of people with integrity, who consciously put spiritual values first, there begins to be something real and true to which those who yearn for the experience of integrity may come. In our own experience, on the basis of our own yearning, we have found something that is of supreme value. We have come to know it to the extent that spiritual values have prevailed in our own living. To this extent there then appears in expression, wherever there are those of integrity who consciously have accepted the supremacy of spiritual values, a means of integration. *Integration* and *integrity* are related words, aren't they? Where there is the reality of integrity known in human living there is a means of integration.

Now, we look around in the world of man and we see a state of disintegration. We see a falling apart and a frantic endeavor to hold it together. People nowadays talk about 'getting it together'. Well, this is what human beings have been trying to do for a long time; this is nothing new. Each generation comes up with a new type of expression but it always says the same old thing because of the state of self-centered consciousness which is shared by human beings the world around. What is known in that state can be described in various ways but it is the state itself that is the point, the self-centered state of human consciousness. It is this which makes disintegration inevitable. With the vast increase of population on earth the illusion of progress begins to be seen for what it is and the inevitability of disintegration becomes apparent. So, blindly and with desperation, there is an endeavor to try to get it all together somehow, to keep it from disintegrating. Now we may see this on the large scale: stresses and strains appear in all directions, and, utilizing the old self-centered methods, the endeavor to keep it together continues, but still it falls apart. We can see it clearly enough also on the smaller scale of the individual. Individually speaking we are inclined to try to keep ourselves together. Why? Well, because we feel that we are falling apart. We have a sense of disintegration and it looks as though that disintegration, being apparently inevitable, requires us to do everything within our power to hold ourselves together. All kinds of methods have been devised to help us to do this. All the various fields of the so-called healing arts are designed to help keep us together, as though it would be disastrous if we actually fell apart and as though it would be disastrous if this supposedly civilized world fell apart. But the world of human construction is based in the consciousness of self-centeredness and this false foundation results inevitably in disintegration.

However, there is the means of integration, but what is to be integrated? Self-centered human beings? The self-centered world of human beings? Is this so important? Is this what is required? We see the evidences of integration on every hand all around us, reaching into the uttermost ends of the universe. It has all been gotten together somehow and it is all held together somehow. Oh, there are those who say that it is flying apart: the galaxies are receding from one another at tremendous speeds. There are all sorts of ideas in this regard, based in the consciousness of self-centeredness, but it is quite evident that the solar system hangs together, and apparently the galaxy itself has been gotten together. Yet human experience is death-oriented; in other words, relates to what is known as disintegration. This is the tragedy, isn't it, of human experience. Disintegration is inevitable, they say. But why? Why? Only because of the state of self-centeredness in man which establishes the inevitability of disintegration.

But are human beings willing to relinquish their self-centeredness? Are they, now? How about us? To what extent have we exhibited a willingness to relinquish self-centeredness in favor of integrity, which puts spiritual values first? Now, of course, many people flirt with the idea and tentatively they may put a foot into the camp of integrity, so to speak, while maintaining the other foot in the camp of self-centeredness. If you do that too long you get split down the middle. A house divided against itself certainly doesn't stand for very long. Now, the foot is held in the camp of self-centeredness, no doubt, for very excellent reasons, according to the self-centered human consciousness. It is thought to be necessary, and certainly to be necessary for one's own satisfaction. But if one is able to convince oneself that it is necessary, one has at the same time convinced oneself that disintegration is necessary. Yet inherently in people there is a feeling that it shouldn't be so; otherwise, why try to get it together so desperately? The disintegration is only consequent upon the persistence of self-centeredness.

Now, obviously, this state of consciousness predominates in the world. Within the scope of the self-centered consciousness there is the good end of the spectrum and the evil end of the spectrum, but it is all self-centeredness and it all contributes to disintegration. Human beings deliberately do those things which bring disintegration in their own experience. The human desire for personal pleasure, personal satisfaction, happiness, the pursuit of happiness – all these things govern what human beings do, and because self-centeredness governs disintegration ensues. Momentarily the individual may feel that there is a little satisfaction here and there in what is done, but it soon palls. In the pattern of self-centeredness, where each individual is in fact basically centered in him- or herself, there is no means of getting it together; there is no true agreement between human beings. Momentarily, again, there may be some apparent surface agreement; people, for instance, get married. But two self-centered people never agree. There may be the appearance of agreement for the moment because on the surface there is agreement self-centeredly about the same things, but pretty soon the cracks begin to appear because there is no basic agreement. Agreement relates to integration, and integration relates to integrity, and integrity is not self-centeredness.

My own personal concern for many years has related to this matter of integrity, and there are those who have recognized this to be true and who have therefore shared this attitude with me. To the extent that we have done so, we have found ourselves to be integrated, not because we chose each other particularly but because we all chose integrity. Giving expression to this reality integrates; we can't help it. You know, this has been proven a fact, because from the standpoint of self-centeredness still remaining in those who were seeking integrity, various likes and dislikes have been present. The idea may be, 'I like this person but I don't like that person.' But to the extent that we were true to integrity, we couldn't get away from each other; whether we liked or disliked made no difference. That's right, isn't it? So that gradually likes and dislikes, which relate to the self-centered state, the materialistic values, cease to be dominant; they don't control anymore. The elements of integrity control and we begin to find ourselves being put together.

Having integrity, our whole approach changes. Obviously, we are in the world the way it is. We are in this self-centered world with human beings in the state of self-centered consciousness. We ourselves know what it is, but in our associations we have a different attitude if we have integrity. We do not go into our associations in the world merely because we think they would be pleasing to us, or, on the other hand, we do not try to get out of associations in the world because we think they would not be pleasing to us. We take it the way it comes because we are not trying to get value for ourselves from the materialistic world around us, we are not trying to get satisfaction from our associations in that world. If we do that, it is obvious that we ourselves have no adequate sense of value. We are looking for it, over here, over there, somewhere else. We are looking for somebody else to give us satisfaction, to make us happy, to be pleasing to 'me'. That's self-centeredness, isn't it? Yet this is the dominating control in the lives of human beings; this is the camp of self-centeredness. There are those who have been associated with the camp of integrity who have tried to keep a foot in each camp. It doesn't work. Finally the individual gets off the fence or it's the end of him. He goes one way or the other, and woe unto those who find themselves sucked back into that self-centered condition!

Those who accept integrity experience value for themselves; and it is this value that they recognize must be brought into all their associations in the world of self-centeredness, so that the fact that they move into any particular pattern of circumstance brings value to that circumstance because they are present. They are not looking for value; they are not looking for pleasure, or satisfaction, or happiness or anything, but are approaching the situation from the standpoint of conveying value into it, conveying integrity into it, so that there is an integrating point in the situation to which there may be response. Now, what can be offered in this regard by a person of integrity will be determined by the level of response; it cannot be arbitrarily imposed. Sometimes, going into a particular situation, there is no external evidence of response at all. Does this mean that nothing can be done? The very fact of the presence of the spirit of integrity is an influence, even though it may be an unconscious influence to most. What can be given in blessing is determined by the extent and the level of response. If response is unconscious, all that can be given is of an unconscious nature. If there is conscious response, something can be given that is of a conscious nature. We have a setting here this morning where there is conscious response, therefore something can be given at the level of that conscious response to the extent of the response.

Very often those who are seeking are seeking self-centeredly. They seek spiritual things self-centeredly. By the way, most of what is called religion in the world has been based in this same self-centered consciousness. Within the scope of Christianity, for instance, the approach is, 'I am a sinner. That's me, you know. I am a sinner.' The question is asked very often, 'Are you saved?' A self-centered approach. 'What's going to happen to me? Poor me! Am I saved? Am I a sinner?' The whole approach is self-centered, lacking integrity.

Integrity is available to the experience of any human being on the face of the earth, because there is something that is true about that person. That person would not exist if it weren't so. Our very existence depends upon the fact that there is something real and true in us, and we find that reality, that truth, when we accept the necessity of behaving with integrity. We cannot behave with integrity until we put spiritual values first – we may say, until we put God first. Now this has meant so many peculiar things to so many people and nothing to most. Put God first. All right, go ahead! Put integrity first; here is our contact with whatever God is. God's character is a character of integrity; everything is integrated. If we do not share that character we have no faintest notion as to what the word *God* might mean. We may have some concepts and beliefs about it, we may get into very heated arguments on this score, but if we find it necessary to argue, it is evidence of the fact that we don't know. We know only through experience, not on the basis of belief. We may believe something; that's fine as a starting point perhaps, if we are willing to relinquish the belief after a while because we move into a larger vision.

We only know through experience. We only know the truth when we actually have integrity and when, of course, consequently our behavior proves it. There is an exemplification of it; spiritual values are put first; God is then put first; we know what it means. But until that experience comes we don't know anything. We have ideas about something, and it is these ideas about things that compose the self-centered consciousness and produce endless conflict of course, because we are all supporting our own particular hangups and they are in conflict with somebody else's hangups, and we get into bloody battles about them, achieving absolutely nothing. Of course, some of the battles are what are called peaceful battles, whatever that would be, peaceful contention. Our whole parliamentary system in this country is based on argument and disagreement. Something good is going to come out of all the disagreement. The system would collapse if we didn't disagree; this is the idea, isn't it? The loyal opposition has to be there opposing. This is the democratic parliamentary system, the system which perpetuates disintegration, not that some other system wouldn't do it too. There are all kinds of systems in the world and they all produce the same result: disintegration.

All that is required is integrity, this one thing. Of course, to start with, a person doesn't really know what that means. 'Take my yoke upon you, and learn of me.' This was the word not only of a very wise man but it is the word of truth. Take the yoke of integrity, placing spiritual values first. You can't place spiritual values first without thinking about it, without paying attention; and to pay attention one has to withdraw attention from the camp of self-centeredness, from what one thought would be pleasing to oneself, from what one thought would be satisfying to one's own experience. One has to withdraw one's attention from one's likes and dislikes, in order to be solely concerned with the matter of integrity, to be right, to discover what it means to be right in any given situation. How many people are interested in that? How many people would even want to talk about it? Mostly because they want to have their own way, they want to do what they want to do. They won't even stop to consider, and if the question, 'Why shouldn't I go in this direction?' is asked, it is merely to find arguments to prove that it is the right direction to go. That isn't honest; that's dishonesty. That has nothing to do with integrity. Integrity is genuine, a genuine desire to discover what it means to express spiritual values. This brings a person, incidentally, out of childishness into maturity. The hallmark of the child is the simple desire to do what he wants to do. That's right, isn't it? The world is peopled by children of all ages, a childishness everywhere, because the self-centeredness reigns supreme and everybody wants to do what they want to do. Of course, we are experts in justifying what we want to do. Oh, we're so good at arguing and convincing ourselves that what we want to do is the right thing to do.

Blessed are those who relinquish that sort of dishonesty and exhibit a willingness to acknowledge the value of integrity, for of such, it may be said, is the kingdom of God – the kingdom of God, the camp of integrity. When there are those of integrity, who are consequently citizens of the kingdom of God, then the kingdom of heaven takes ζQ form on earth. The word *kingdom* relates, of course, to government and control. Integrity governs and controls, and because of that, the truth that heaven and earth are one becomes apparent. Value is no longer given to material things but rather to the spiritual reality, and then material things reveal their true value because they have true value in oneness with spiritual values. As we are willing to participate in this, people of inherent integrity come; they cannot help themselves. They come regardless of likes and dislikes. In spite of themselves they come, because the integrating force is at work putting things together in the true design, in the right way, under the dominion of God. We see this occurring within the scope of our own experience, both with respect to ourselves as individuals and with respect to those who come. They do not come to enrol in an organization; they come to participate in the creation of a living organism. My word for many, many years has been, 'Who will share with me the responsibilities of this building?' And there are those who have come and do share in it. In the process of coming, of course, there tends to be a building with one hand and a tearing down with the other, but eventually it becomes building. There are those who have persisted in the tearing down on the one hand because they had a foot in the camp of self-centeredness, but gradually building begins to predominate because integrity begins to predominate. And where there is integrity there is integration, and nobody can stop it. It works. It is working. All things work together to perfection!

The Most High

'He that dwelleth in the secret place of the most High shall abide under the shadow of the Almighty.'

The place of the most High has been secret in human experience. It is not actually hidden; it is not meant to be obscure; it is really the natural place for a person to be. However, to know it, what is really most High must be most high to the person who thus knows the secret place; then, of course, it isn't secret. One may always wisely question as to what is most high in one's own attitude, in one's own living. Whatever is put in the highest position establishes a state which is not secret to the person who experiences it. Whatever is put in the highest position is to that person God. Whatever is put in the highest position will determine how the individual behaves. It is not as though nothing is in that highest position. It is not as though human beings do not know how to worship before the god whom they place in that position. It is being done constantly by everyone; there is always something most high for the person in the moment.

Usually when God is mentioned, and a person has some belief in God, the attitude is taken that God is in the highest position; but the momentary functions in living actually tell the tale. So much of human assumption is just that; it is imagination. There are, no doubt, many people on the face of the earth who say they believe in God but in fact they don't, because behavior in the moment will reveal what is being put at the point of the most high. I suppose it could be said that they believe in god spelt with a little *g*, the particular idol of the moment. The customary state of human beings is that of idolatry. What is put at the place of the most high in human experience is seldom the reality implied by the word *God*.

If you pause to consider in any given moment as to what you are

88

then placing at the point of the most high in relationship to yourself you will have to admit that there are many strange gods. Acquisitiveness, or greed, is obviously in the most high place for many people. Whatever will support this endeavor, this attitude in themselves, will control in the moment. The desire for pleasure, for some sort of self-satisfaction, self-gratification of one kind or another, is most frequently at the most high point in human experience. That, then, is the god for the person; that, then, will determine the individual's attitude and the individual's behavior, what he will do, how he will act, what words will be expressed. While emphasis does not need to be laid too much upon the matter, it might be profitable, in passing, to list all the various things that are in their seasons placed at the most high point in your own experience. And you will likely find, if you are honest, that you have a great range of false gods, even though in the general sense you may say, 'The true God is at the point of the most high in me. I love God. I serve God.' Do you really?

Whatever the most high is in the moment in your own place of worship, that place will not be secret to you. It will be what you are in the moment. It will determine the revelation of you – either a false you, or, if it is the true God, then the true you. This is obvious enough to anyone who really looks at it. Again, I would suggest that it can be profitable to be honest in examining what you place at the most high point in your own momentary living – not in the imaginary view of your life expression but in what actually happens, because it is this that counts. The imagination means nothing in this regard; it is what actually occurs that tells the tale.

'He that dwelleth in the secret place of the most High shall abide under the shadow of the Almighty.' Now there is One who is actually most High; there is that which belongs in the most high position in one's own attitude, something real rather than something imaginary. 'He that dwelleth in the secret place of the most High shall abide under the shadow of the Almighty.' The shadow of the Almighty implies protection, for one thing, but it also indicates an inclusion in the very nature of the Almighty. All who dwell in the secret place of the most High share the experience of being under the shadow of the Almighty; in other words, they are together, they are together in the experience of whatever the shadow of the Almighty may be. Another thing it implies is the presence of the Almighty; something must be present if a shadow is cast. So there is a dwelling in the secret place of the most High and an abiding in the presence of the Almighty.

Those who believe in God may be hopeful that they are in the presence of God, that He is on hand and somehow on the lookout for them. But who really knows it? To whom is it more than a hope? Someone may say, 'I have faith.' In what? Human beings have faith in whatever they place at the high point; they have faith in what is most high to them in the moment, obviously so. It is imagined that whatever is put as being most high will provide the most satisfactory experience in the moment. Of course this is not always what is actually experienced; sometimes fear is placed at the most high point. Whatever it is that is most high governs in the individual life, and fear does govern on occasion, doesn't it? – a false god. Fear is present when the experience of the true God is absent. There is a gap and the individual is very much aware of the gap and fear consequently is known. A false god is being placed in the position of the most high in the immediate experience.

Most of our experiences day by day are looked upon usually as being more or less humdrum, nothing too outstanding, more or less routine. What would you say the percentage of routineness is in your present experience day by day? Ninety percent? Ninety-five percent? Ninety-eight percent? Occasionally something out of the ordinary happens. The out-of-the-ordinary happening seems in most instances to be something that is disturbing. Of course, if the most high god of the moment relates to what one supposes will bring the greatest pleasure, then this may be looked upon as a pleasing experience, and there are some outstandingly pleasing experiences of this nature, no doubt. But whether it is pleasing or whether it is disturbing, it is all consequent upon the worship of a false god; it is all consequent upon placing something at the most high position that doesn't belong there.

In view of the fact that most of human experience is looked upon as being more or less routine – this is the largest area – then it should receive the most attention presumably. So many people live from weekend to weekend – no wonder their state is a weak end! – in other words, from the most high to the most high in their own con-

sciousness. A weekend is not a very satisfactory god; just to get
through what is in between occupies a good deal of human endeavor:
get through it without noticing it, if possible, and then live it up on
the weekend. What an appalling existence! What a meaningless state!
What a pattern of ignorant stupidity! This is conceived by many to
be the highest fulfilment in life. Nonsense. It's an indication of childish self-centeredness. It is the indication of a failure to place what
really is most High in the position of the most high; and unless one
does that, one is living a false life and that is no life at all, which is
proven out in season.

True life is only known when what is at the position of the most
high is what belongs there, the most High – what is really most high,
not what is imagined to be most high in one's own personal experience. Perhaps we can see how the religious idea of a personal Saviour
comes into the picture, because certainly that which belongs at the
point of the most high should be placed there in a personal sense; one
has to let it be so for oneself if it is to have any meaning. The idea
with many is to put Jesus at that point. But how would you do that,
except in imagination? The most High is not really imaginary. The
most High is not merely something to be believed in or hoped for.
Here is the one true reality insofar as a person is concerned; everything else is unreal, imaginary, until the reality is placed at the point
of the most high. Nearly everyone lives a completely imaginary life.
It's an existence that has no substance. And most feel that there isn't
much substance to it, so they try to fill it out some way. Some people
try to fill it out with food. 'Eat, drink and be merry, for tomorrow we
die.' No, we're dead today!

'He that dwelleth in the secret place of the most High shall abide
under the shadow of the Almighty,' shall find himself to be a part
of the reality of being, no longer fooling around in an imaginary
state. We often speak of children's imagination, don't we? Children
are very much inclined to live in an imaginary world. Most people
never grow up. They take their imaginary world with them because
they have imaginary things in the position of the most high in their
own attitudes and experience.

The most High. What is the reality? Perhaps we touch that reality
in the first instance in a recognition of something of the true quality

of character, we may say of the character of God, but if we leave it as the character of God it doesn't mean very much. It is only when we begin to associate ourselves with that character that it takes on some substance. Those who gaze into the high heavens to see God may have a vivid imagination in that regard and perhaps recognize something that is true of the character of God, but it stays so far away from them. There is very little sense of relatedness in such case and the individual, instead of abiding under the shadow of the Almighty, abides in the condition of a sinner, abides in the condition of being merely human, abides in the state of imperfection. The state of imperfection is looked upon as being the normal condition of human beings, oneself particularly. It provides an excuse: 'Well, I can't help it because I am not perfect, you know.' How convenient, one always has a ready-made excuse for failure. Human beings are thoroughly wedded to failure. This has little to do with the shadow of the Almighty, certainly, and consequently there is evidence of a very inadequate, at best, dwelling in the secret place of the most High.

But when we do begin to put the true character of God at the most high position in our own experience, then something real begins to emerge, something that has substance. We begin to discover that we are not exactly what we thought we were before. There is movement toward the experience of a new identity. Now, this shouldn't seem so peculiar, because, after all, we have had quite a number of identities along the way. We had a baby identity once – you probably don't remember too much about that one because it wasn't too clearly in focus yet. Then we had a childhood identity, an adolescent identity. Some of us even have adult identity but not, as we have noted before, necessarily a mature identity. There is a changing pattern in this regard which is largely based in a changing outlook, a changing experience of ourselves. If, coming to adulthood, we think we have got it made now, we merely fool ourselves. Only those who have learned what it means to dwell in the secret place of the most High abide under the shadow of the Almighty, where the true nature of being is. If the shadow of the Almighty is not known, a person doesn't know himself, and there is no way to become aware of the shadow of the Almighty, which is present in any case, except by dwelling in the secret place of the most High, except by placing at the high point in one's own living what belongs there, so that one keeps his integrity. And it is not a matter of putting all these other false gods at the high point.

We do this in our momentary existence: we can either place a false god at the high point or we can allow the reality to be there in our own experience. The reality is there anyway but we can shut ourselves off from it, we can fail to be aware of it, and we can go on our own not-so-sweet way. The reality is present and it takes a deliberate action on the part of a human being to put something else at the high point that doesn't belong there. Most people think of the deliberate action as being the opposite, don't they? But because something false has been deliberately put at the high point, it takes some deliberate action to let it go. But it is in the letting go of it that the awareness of the reality becomes possible, because as long as we are holding a false god in the position of the most high, that's all we see. It is impossible to say, 'Now, I am going to keep this false god there for a while because I am not so sure of this reality yet; so I'll keep the false god here and I'll look over there for the reality.' But the reality is where you put the false god, and as long as you have the false god there, the awareness and experience of the reality is impossible.

How enthusiastically human beings maintain at the high point of their own experience all the things that don't belong there, all the things of self-centeredness, basically all the things that the individual thinks would be pleasing to him- or herself. 'Let these things govern; let these things determine what my choice and my attitude are going to be in any circumstance.' That is dwelling in the not-so-secret place of the most low, and it brings a very low state, a filthy state. This is the way human beings behave, isn't it? But we have begun to see the necessity of letting the reality be present in our own experience. We can't really put it there. Are you going to get hold of God and say, 'Now, God, I want you here'? God is there already but hidden behind a dark veil, usually of the most low. We may become aware that the reality is present, that the qualities of true being are present. We couldn't have any awareness of the nature of those qualities if they weren't present. They are not going to come from somewhere. They are not even invisible now. They are present now; to the extent of our awareness of them we know that they are present. When we begin to put such things where they belong in our own awareness, then we are agreeing with the truth, because they are there already; they are in the place where they belong. But when we acknowledge that they are in the place where they belong, then we begin to be true to ourselves.

We do this in the moment, not at the points of crisis or climax; because if we haven't been doing it in the routine moments of our living we won't do it in the exceptional moments. We will find ourselves involved with the most low. When some critical experience arises in your living, how do you handle it? From what standpoint do you handle it? From the standpoint of the reality that is most high or from the standpoint of what you have been placing in that position during the routine moments of your existence? If you are not experiencing what it means to be yourself, a real person, in the routine moments of your living, you will not have that experience to take into the critical moments of your living. You may, in the routine moments, be able to fool yourself, to float along more or less; but let something critical arise and see what happens. When those critical moments arose for Job, what was his attitude? 'The Lord gave, and the Lord hath taken away; blessed be the name of the Lord.' But what would be the attitude of a person who had placed things which don't belong at the high point, in his routine experience? 'How is this going to affect me? What are people going to think? How can I use the situation to my own advantage?'

There are a number of instances recorded in the stories, in the Old Testament particularly, when a servant of the Lord was faced with something especially difficult, when there was, as in the case of Job, some disaster at hand. You will note that in each instance basically the same attitude was always taken as was summarized in those words spoken by Job, 'The Lord gave, and the Lord hath taken away; blessed be the name of the Lord.' This situation is occurring, whatever it is, because of the working of the creative power of God in the circumstances as they are here on earth, with human beings behaving the way they do. Everything that occurs is on this basis. Are we going to object, then, and say to God, 'Stop Your power working; it's making things difficult here'? Well, we may say that, and some people think that's prayer. 'Stop it, God, hold everything; I don't like it.' But it doesn't stop. This is the irresistible force we were talking

about. It is futile to try to resist it. Let it work and the results of its
working will be exactly as they should be according to the attitudes
and the ways, the behaviour, of human beings and all that is present
round about. So there is no need to object or rebel. The Lord giveth
and the Lord taketh away; blessed be the name of the Lord. Good,
this is wonderful! It may be used to advantage, but not for the individual; to the advantage of the purposes of God. When we have
this attitude we know that all things are in fact used to the advantage
of the purposes of God, and we may align ourselves with that.

An outstanding example of someone who was aligned with the
purposes of God is seen in Moses when he came to the Red Sea.
There are those who imagine that somehow Moses was granted some
special power – if this really happened, mind you – so that when he
held out his rod or his hand, whatever it was, then, because of that,
the Red Sea parted. No, he was the right man at the right time, in the
right place. He was with what was moving, and something was really
moving then. So that circumstance was used to advantage, the advantage of the purposes of God. In self-centeredness the Israelites may
have thought this was especially for them: 'We're so important, you
know, God had to save us.' Well, they had some importance, but not
in a self-centered sense. They were important to the purposes of God.
Because Moses was on hand and was moving with it, it all worked
out. The irresistible force was made evident in the experience of
those concerned, in a constructive way insofar as the children of
Israel were concerned. It wasn't so good for the Egyptians. And why
wasn't it so good for the Egyptians? Because they were moving on the
basis of something false at the position of the most high. That something false was Pharaoh, for one thing – not that Pharaoh needed to
be false, but he proved himself to be that way.

It is what we do in our momentary living that counts. If we have
the experience of being ourselves in the true sense, in handling our
momentary affairs, then we have this foundation when circumstances
intensify and the critical points arise. But if we do not take advantage
of being true in what is looked upon as being routine, we are going to
be in trouble at the critical points. The habit of being ourselves must
be established, and it is established in the ninety percent or ninety-
five percent or ninety-eight percent of our experience, not in the little

percentage that is left. It is what we do consistently moment by moment by moment that determines what is so, that determines whether we are dwelling in the secret place of the most High. The statement is not, 'Call in to the secret place of the most High once a week, and you may do it by telephone if you want.' No, that's not the statement at all. Be there, dwell there, stay there, be consistent! This is one of the characteristics of God, one we can be most thankful for. He is consistent; He doesn't change His mind all the time. And let's not try to make Him change His mind either. There's nothing wrong with His mind; there's something wrong with ours if we try to make Him change His.

So we have opportunity, all of us, to move into the situation of the moment in a consciousness of who we are, in a consciousness of divine being, so that our outlook is from the divine standpoint and our behavior is true to what we are. This is more important than anything, when we have placed at the position of the most high what belongs there. We do not anymore proceed on the basis of expediency, looking for personal advantage, advantage in the way of getting something that we think would be satisfying to ourselves. That's a false god. Let us dwell in the secret place of the most High, and as we do this, as it becomes the consistent experience in the routine affairs day by day, we discover what is implied by the words 'abiding under the shadow of the Almighty' – the all-mighty.

I mentioned Moses and the Red Sea. Here was something that gave evidence of the Almighty. The almightiness of God is constantly at work. Let us let it emerge into our own experience so that we don't keep it hidden by this thick blackness which is always there when we worship false gods, when we place things at the high point in our own attitudes that don't belong there. When we do that, we betray ourselves and, at the same time, we betray everybody else. This is something that each person must do for himself. Here is where that 'personal Saviour' bit comes in. Is one going to be honest and acknowledge what now is actually at the high point, or is one going to deny and betray that? That is the question that is being asked of everybody. Are you going to be true to the truth? Are you going to be true to what is now at the high point in you, the reality that is there, or are you going to try to put something else at that point and behave accordingly? There it is, and the person who puts something else at the high point that doesn't belong there is in bad trouble. This is why the world of mankind is in bad trouble, because everything else under the sun has been put at that high point. Of course it all comes to focus in the self-centeredness of man, what he wants for himself.

'He that dwelleth in the secret place of the most High,' he who abides there consistently, he who acknowledges what is at that high point in himself, behaving accordingly, 'shall abide under the shadow of the Almighty.' That is the truth!

Values

The sense of loneliness is consequent upon man's loss of the consciousness of his own true value. It may be said that man, male and female, has been unconscious both of the individual reality of being and of the value of the reality of being of mankind. Who has an awareness – and I am not talking about an intellectual concept or idea or belief, but an actual awareness – of the reason for the existence of mankind? Or, coming back to the individual, the reason for one's own existence? Because the real value of oneself has been obscured there is a consequent sense of void and emptiness, isolation, loneliness. This is present in the whole body of mankind and in all individuals. Because of it, as we noted this morning, there is the endeavor to use other people and things to assuage the loneliness: the collection of toys and teddy bears that are deemed to be necessary to satisfy the childish human being. People become very much incensed if their teddy bears should be threatened.

Throughout the whole world there is a collection of false systems of value. To describe it in allegorical terms, some people favor teddy bears, others gollywogs, or what have you. There are a multitude of different systems of value. The particular system of value in the United States, for instance, is very different from the system of value in Vietnam. Everybody is inclined to look at everybody else from the standpoint of their own particular system of value. Now these various systems of value cannot be arbitrarily changed (although this has been the endeavor on the part of different countries from time to time) because they are developed over a long period of time. As I say, there are a multitude of these systems of value throughout the whole world, developed by different people as being satisfactory, as far as this might be possible, in filling the apparent needs and voids of those concerned.

The idea is that, because of the sense of isolation and loneliness, one must find something to fill this void, and the way this is done develops and produces a system of value for a particular people. But you will note it is all done on a self-centered basis, to find those things which will, after a fashion at least, satisfy the people concerned, make them feel less lonely, less isolated. The approach, then, is fundamentally a self-centered one, and the things which achieve the desired end, as much as they do, are thought of as having value. These things have value because they seem, for the moment at least, to provide a certain satisfaction insofar as the empty experience of the particular people is concerned. Now, this inevitably varies from people to people according to the character of the people, and this relates also to the area where they live. We all find ourselves embedded in these systems of value.

The same thing in a little different way is true from individual to individual. Within the scope of the collective system of value, the individual develops his own methods of satisfying and covering up as far as possible his sense of loneliness and emptiness. From the environment, from other people, each person tends to be on the grab to find those things which will seemingly fill the need. All this is related to what are called human needs, but human needs are merely the evidence of the failure of human beings to experience the truth of their own value, the truth of themselves, the reality of their own being. Because this has not been known in mind, in consciousness, and in physical manifestation, the individual feels lost. This is true of every person on the face of the earth: that sense of loss is there even though it may be covered up to a certain extent by these various systems of value and by the individual methods developed to try to take care of the uncomfortable condition. In order to fill the void the individual may have to have this or that; he may have to – in his own view at least – have this or that relationship with somebody else.

All these systems of value and all these methods that human beings use individually to try to take care of a bad situation are in direct conflict with the way by which the truth might be experienced. Obviously, if a person does develop a very fine means of covering up his own loneliness and making himself feel that he has some value and that he is important somehow, if he succeeds in doing this, then he is thoroughly self-deceived, because on such a basis he has prevented himself from experiencing the truth of himself and substituted a human endeavor to fill human needs. The world around, people are very much concerned with what are called human needs. Of course, these needs are very often simply physical needs: people are hungry, people are starving; they have to be fed. These are considered to be the primary needs. But when things get to an extreme of this sort it is consequent upon the original failure of human beings to become aware of, to be reacquainted with, the truth of themselves.

The constant endeavor to fill so-called human needs is a constant endeavor to defeat God or to defeat the reality of being. Man has been very hopeful that he could do this, that he could design his world in such a way that all human needs would be taken care of. But this would be man in complete isolation, with no consciousness whatsoever of any relatedness to anything beyond his own kind. As we noted this morning, if he could dispense with nature he would do it. If he could get along all right, all self-contained for man himself, then to hell with nature! Here is the thoroughly self-centered, selfish attitude which has become universal in the human race, and it is considered to be normal and natural. Far from it! It is the evidence of the fact that man has moved into a state of virtual oblivion insofar as his own reality is concerned, and the fact of oblivion may well put in an appearance one day. It does individually anyway, but it could do it for the whole of mankind, simply because he has his back to the truth.

He has his back to the truth as long as he is trying to fill his own needs. What a heretical statement; because, after all, virtually all the energy of all people everywhere is directed toward filling the needs of human beings, and it seems to the self-centered view to be utterly impractical and suicidal, indeed, not to have the attitude which necessitates the filling of human needs. This is an indication of how far from an understanding of the truth human beings have gone, how blind and ignorant they have become. In spite of all the ballyhoo about progress, I doubt if mankind has ever been more ignorant. Oh, they know a lot about many things but in fact know the reality of virtually nothing.

The systems of value that human beings have developed have been produced on a self-centered basis. Now, there are some who earnestly endeavor to harmonize the various systems of value. This is considered to be the way by which we might have peace on earth, because, obviously, these various systems of value come into conflict with each other and fundamentally nobody understands anybody else. Nobody can understand anybody else on the basis of a false system of value. If it is possible to have false systems of value, there is an implication that there must be a true system of value. What is the difference between the true system of value and all the false systems of value? As we have noted, value is given to things which seem to be of benefit to man, which seem to fill his voids, his needs, that seem to reduce his sense of loneliness, so that things apparently do not have any value until they do something for the benefit of man. This establishes the nature of a false system of value. The true system of value has value; it doesn't need to be given value by human beings. If it is necessary to give value to something it is an indication of a false value. If we take some item that seems to be very important to human beings, we will say some particular relationship with somebody, and say, 'Well, that relationship is valuable because it fills a need in the human being concerned,' that is a false value. People everywhere, of course, are shopping around here, there and everywhere to find the things that are going to fill what they conceive to be their needs.

Now the fundamental needs are internal, one might say (I am not speaking about the stomach), but relate to this sense of aloneness, aloneness because the truth has been lost, the truth which is a part of the universal whole. Being conscious of the truth of one's own being immediately brings the sense of relatedness to everything. That sense of relatedness has dissipated loneliness then. Loneliness is thought of as being something external – I am lonely because I have no friends; I am lonely because I seem to be isolated. No, that is not the reason for loneliness. If it is assumed that that is the reason for loneliness, then of course the person will get busy and try to get friends; and there is the attitude on the part of so many, 'Well, I need love.' So this futile endeavor to fill oneself up with what is assumed to be necessary to take care of the uncomfortable internal state occupies so much attention that very few people ever realize there is any other way of functioning.

This endeavor, to clothe it in its true terms, could be defined by using the word *greed*. Of course, nowadays people have all kinds of nice fancy names to describe these rotten things so as to make them look good. They are described very often in social terms. Nowadays we must have a social consciousness, which is another way of saying we must be self-centered, we must be selfish, we must be greedy. Greediness is excused by using fancy words, very often, to describe it; but if anyone looks honestly at the scene of things he can see everybody on the grab – me, me, me! And in order to satisfy me I will combine with you, you and you and we will satisfy all of us. Power! All this talk about power is simply selfishness, greed. Of course, it is excused – 'Oh, we are being so unjustly treated,' and self-pity is a prime motivation. Of course, it's not called that: 'fairness and justice.' Dishonesty!

So, beginning to see things as they really are, we may recognize that there is a true system of value; at least we can call it that. This relates to God, or the reality that has been described by that word. If God – whatever that word means – is a reality, then does that reality have value already or does it only take on value when man gives it value? It may be said that it only takes on value for man when he gives it value, but in fact it already has value; it is not made any more valuable by man giving it value. I think sometimes the idea has been given that God is somehow on the grab: He wants love from you, you and you, and the more the better. But this is merely what human beings see of their own reflection; it has nothing to do with the reality. The reality already has value; it's not on the grab to try to get it. Here is the distinction: the true values have value which is not produced by man, because what is produced by man is all related to what is seemingly for the benefit of man, and the reality which God is is not particularly for the benefit of man.

This reality relates to the truth of what man really is, of what you and I really are. This is something invisible, or not found by the examination of external things. Most of man's interests have been directed toward the examination of external things. The end result of that is nothing. He really finds nothing, because the reality is not the external thing. The external things give evidence of the fact that there is a reality, just as your living body gives evidence of the fact that there is the reality of life. But no amount of probing into your body will discover what life is; in fact, the more you probe the less life you will have, and if you probe too far the life's gone. Yet that's not the way to put it, really; that's not the truth of the matter. The life isn't gone; the form has been separated from the life and ceases to be of any value.

The physical form of anything, including man, has a potential of value because it may reveal what already has value. You as an individual, in your reality, already have value; you do not have to get value. But it is evident that from the standpoint of your body and your consciousness there has been an inadequate experience of that value which you are. To experience that value, of course, it must be expressed. The consciousness of the body and the body itself provide the facility by which the expression may appear, and when the expression does appear the voids are filled. There is the experience of the reality of oneself, and that experience is not separate from the reality of anything else throughout the whole universe, so where would the loneliness be? No more loneliness; not because someone else filled a need in you, not because you got a nice new shiny car to fill a need in yourself, not because you married a wife or took a husband to fill a need in yourself, but because you yourself took responsibility for expressing the reality of yourself, and that is sufficient.

When the reality is expressed through the facilities that are available to let it happen, then the environment begins to reflect that reality and the proper relationships appear. As we well know, the world as it now is is simply a reflection of the state of man. Man lost — the world lost. Man in confusion inside himself — the world in confusion. To try to sort out the world and make it not confused is the most senseless and useless and futile undertaking. What needs to be sorted out is man, and there is only one man insofar as each person is concerned, sometimes male and sometimes female. Unless the change comes there, in oneself, it will come nowhere else; yet how much attention is paid to this? 'Oh, no, we're going to elect a government; now perhaps a minority government will be good in Canada because they will really have to toe the mark.' To do what? 'Oh, to fill the

needs of all of us – won't that be nice – so that we will have everything we want and all the voids in us will be filled to the brim, social
security and all.' But how many secure people are there in the world?
What nonsense!

The only way that any voids in the world can be filled is through a
person who allows the voids in himself to be filled and does not
require his environment or someone else to do it. He expresses the
truth of his own being, and that truth is a part of the true system of
value. If – and this is idle speculation at the moment – everybody on
the face of the earth undertook to let this happen, there would be only
one system of value; no basis for conflict therefore. Now, looking at it
this way, people say, 'Well, the undertaking is quite futile because
people are simply not going to let it happen.' That's true with most,
but perchance there is one person here and another person there and
someone else further over who might be willing to let it happen, who
took the responsibility of letting it happen. I trust that some of these
people are here present this evening, because when the true values
begin to find a means of expression on earth, even though it seems to
be small, it is infinitely more powerful than anything that might
appear through the false systems of value. Something begins to
happen; not in the ways of men, not on the basis of the systems of
false value. If you try to make things work out on the basis of these
systems, any of them, it is sure to fail. But there is a true system
of value and we may begin to be a means by which this may
be expressed in our living. Never mind anybody else; there
are plenty of people who are trying to make everybody else live
some way, according to some system of value, and dying in the
attempt. Never mind anybody else, just accept the responsibility for
yourself.

Of course, this was beautifully, clearly, vividly, demonstrated quite
some time ago by a man called Jesus. He took the responsibility
Himself. Everybody has said, 'Oh, nobody else could do that; nobody
else could take that responsibility.' No, they couldn't take His responsibility. Of course not. You can't take anybody else's responsibility. But each person is quite capable of taking his or her own.
That is exactly what we are here to do, when we are honest with
ourselves: to express the character that is a revelation of the already

existing true values. This character is available to be expressed by anyone in whom life is still present.

When there is hungering and thirsting for this, to be true to one's own integrity, to be honorable in the expression of what is right, then the addictions to all these other things which have been used to try to satisfy one's own lacks can no longer control. As we noted this morning, people are addicted to everything under the sun. It is not just a matter of alcohol and drugs. My goodness, no. There would be no problem with alcohol and drugs if people everywhere weren't already addicted. One could say they are addicted to what has been called the forbidden fruit: trying to satisfy oneself, trying to fill one's own seeming needs, the empty places in oneself, by extracting what possibly may be valuable out of the world around to do this. That is eating of the forbidden fruit. That is what brings death and all that leads to death, the decreasing experience of life. So we need to emerge out of our addictions. And do you know that there are many addictions which people don't realize as being addictions? One can be addicted to something good, you know. In fact, whenever a person becomes addicted to anything, he does it because he thinks at the time that it is good. He wouldn't act in that field if he didn't think it was good. 'It is going to be good' – taking the extremes – 'if I drink a bottle of wine,' and someone may become an alcoholic.

Now, the alcoholics have an organization, called Alcoholics Anonymous, that is designed to help the individual out of that particular addiction; but it is said that once an alcoholic, always an alcoholic. Strictly speaking, that isn't true, but it is true in relationship to the method used to control the addiction. It doesn't clear the addiction; it merely controls it. The addiction is still there. Nothing has changed, actually. The way of control is to substitute one addiction for another, so people become addicted to Alcoholics Anonymous, and to the extent that they are so addicted they cannot clear from addiction, either to alcohol or Alcoholics Anonymous. This is the way that addictions are controlled very often in the world of false values: by substituting a better addiction for a worse addiction. But they are all still addictions; they are all still related to filling the need in the person from an external source. If an addiction is to be cleared in fact – and fundamentally the addiction that needs to be cleared is the eating of the forbidden fruit — it is because there is an acceptance of true values, so that one is no longer controlled, governed, by the false values, by the system of false value in the general sense or by the personal system that one has established for oneself, the personal addictions that one has accepted for oneself.

One of the addictions which seems to be a very good one, to which a lot of people are subject, is the human idea about justice: the endeavor to establish a state of justice in the external sense and to feel very righteous if the individual's sense of justice is violated. There are a lot of people in the world crying out, 'Injustice, injustice,' usually on the basis of 'I am being treated unjustly,' or a minority is being treated unjustly. Therefore, being addicted to a concept about justice, the individual is governed in his life accordingly, and he tries to fill what he conceives is the need in this regard. So he waves his flag and gets busy and tries to make the world over so that it will be a just place. But the world can never be a just place as long as there are false systems of value. Of course, as long as there are false systems of value there will also be conflicting false systems of value. Justice only begins to emerge into actual experience, so that a person knows what it is, when there is the expression in living of the true values, one's own true nature, the nature which characterizes the source of all that has appeared in the whole universal structure.

Should we consider ourselves to be exempt from allowing this character to appear through us? This is the attitude that human beings have taken: 'Oh, we don't need that! We are going to set up our own systems of value and we are going to get things to work the way we want them to work.' Is it any wonder that people feel isolated? This attitude isolates everybody from the whole universe, and then everybody is convinced that we live in a hostile universe bent on our destruction and it is only by reason of our valor that we are able to survive at all. What nonsense! It's only by the mercy of God that we have been able to survive at all, only by reason of the fact that we still have a little life. What is the true character of that life? When we begin to align ourselves with that, then we find that nothing is hostile; there is nothing whatsoever bent on our destruction. Of course, this idea of hostility and destruction merely appears to man to be this way because man, in his forgetfulness of the reality of his own being, has become a hostile and destructive creature and he sees that reflected in his environment. But it is his own reflection; it isn't the nature of anything around him; it is what is around him reflecting his own nature.

Man has responsibility for what is around him, and when we come back into position to reveal in our own living the true values, then the environment reflects that and there is no sweat. How much sweat of the face there is in the world consequent upon the eating of the forbidden fruit! This is a beautiful story because it tells it like it is. It's not just a religious fancy; it's a story of fact, couched in these particular terms but nevertheless true. How much sweat of the face there is in the world; everything that man does is a pain in the neck. Oh, what effort . . . vast sums of money, tremendous effort. 'Develop machines to give us more power to do what we want to do.' Did you ever observe a tree growing? Actually, there is a tremendous amount of power there. Think of all that substance being lifted up and held there. How long would you like to hold your arm out this way? Yet here is something quietly happening, no big noise about it, just in one tree. How many trees are there on earth? It seems nowadays that the number is being reduced, but there are still quite a number. And all this is happening so easily, so naturally, no problem. But anything that man does, oh, the problems! He thinks he solves one problem, but in solving that one problem – according to his view at least – it has produced another ten problems, so then he has to go after these ten. The more problems he solves the more problems he has, because he is trying to bulldoze – that's a good word, isn't it; the bulldozer is a very popular instrument these days – his own way, regardless of anything, to satisfy himself and his own needs. He is greedy and selfish and, insofar as the universe is concerned, useless. He is bent on his own ends – that's a good way of describing it – and so the end comes.

But any end may also be a beginning. This moment is an end and this moment is also a beginning. In this moment the acceptance of responsibility can be known by anyone, the responsibility for finding and expressing the truth of one's own being. When a person longs for this above all else, it may be experienced. But if he is still intent on his addictions, on trying to fill himself up with what he thinks is necessary to satisfy himself, he will know nothing, he will never discover anything. We have a lot of lukewarm people who pay a little attention on occasion to what they deem to be spiritual things, but where are those with integrity who have this burning desire to be right in the expression of life, to reveal the true character, uninfluenced, uncontrolled, by all these things round about, regardless of the situation, regardless of present relationships or anything else? – just to be right, to express what is right. What a shattering thing! But the minute anyone begins to let this happen, things change. Now, of course, when things begin to change, a person is inclined to look at what is changing and say, 'Well, I didn't expect this to happen. I don't like this much. It doesn't conform with my system of value.' To hell with your system of value! What about the true system of value? Who knows that? We don't know it until we begin to express it, and we don't know what effect it is going to have, so don't judge the effects; let them be whatever they are. Be consistent, honest, keep your integrity, in the expression of the true qualities and values of which you become increasingly aware when you express them.

People want to have things handed to them on a platter: 'Well, you tell me; tell me all this and then I will know.' Oh no you won't. The only way you can know is by doing it yourself, by letting it happen in your own experience so that what is needed in the moment in the expression of those values may take form through you. When it does, it will have an effect. Good! – whatever the effect is. How do you know what the effect should be? There may be some ultimate idea of a heaven on earth somewhere. Well, if it is just a vague idea, leave it that way. Don't try to be specific, because at this point nobody knows, and it is this propensity of human beings to imagine that they know, when they don't, that messes things up. Just be concerned with the expression of the true values and let the chips fall where they may, and they will fall in the true design; they will begin to reflect the true values, and that's beautiful. But to reach from the point of initiation to the point of culmination there has to be the traversing of the intervening territory. A babe is not born the moment it is conceived. It passes through many changes, some of them not so beautiful apparently, if one were there to see it. Wisely, it's hidden. Of course man has gotten busy and opened things up and looked and said, 'Well, it works this way and this way and this way.' Does that make it work any better? It was working fine before he ever looked. Leave things alone and stop trying to make things work the way some human being in his particular system of value thinks they should work. Look at the conflict there is in the world on this basis.

Let us yield to the true values and take the responsibility just of expressing those values, not of trying to convert someone else to some belief or other; to inspire perhaps, to encourage, to assist people to be true to themselves, to express the real values themselves regardless of where they are, in what situation. Whether it seems to be unfair or just or whatever, it doesn't matter. Whatever the situation may be, the truth, the reality, may be expressed, and this is the real value. Where the real value is expressed the evidence of that value appears; you can't stop it. It appears just as surely as the evidence of false values appears when they are expressed. We should have plenty of awareness in this regard; there is evidence on every hand. All right, let's change the picture, not expect someone else to change it; certainly don't expect the government to change it. The government is the central core of a particular system of value; they are not going to change anything in the right way. But take the responsibility of doing it yourself, letting it happen because you are on earth. You don't need to lead a political party to do that; in fact, if you start leading a political party you will mess things up. Just express the reality of being and the job gets done!

Man at the Core

There are those on the face of the earth, you included presumably, who have begun to recognize what is taking place and have consequently assumed a certain responsibility thereto. The mists of consciousness clear, the light shines, and we begin to comprehend what our purpose is, what the purpose of God is, and the manner of its achievement.

This awareness comes, not because there is the endeavor to try to understand or to figure it all out but because there is an exhibited willingness to move with the creative cycles that are at work. In that movement, we find ourselves being changed and restored to a different state, a state which is new to us. Because of its newness it has heretofore been unknown, and therefore there may tend to be some trepidation, an understandable trepidation; and yet this fearful attitude is often used as an excuse for resisting the process in our own experience. Obviously there is a need to learn to trust, so that even though there may be some uncertainty, some fear even, involved, we do not give it any weight in our own attitudes, because we have learned to trust the Lord.

Such trust is essential, because it is quite impossible to comprehend, even to see, everything that is working out. Fortunately, what is occurring does not have to be directed by our human minds. We have been accustomed to trying to direct things on this basis heretofore, perhaps, and it is this that has produced the confusion and the turmoil in our world. Presumably we have been reaching a point where, seeing this, we finally exhibit a willingness to trust the Lord so that whatever is to occur may remain in His hands insofar as we are concerned. The fact of the matter is that everything is in His hands; the creative process is working and will move in its appointed cycles to the ultimate conclusion. Using the word *conclusion,* I refer to the re-creation or restoration that is the immediate divine purpose.

How that purpose works out in the experience of human beings is a question, but that it will work out is not a question. Human experience remains a question because each individual must determine his own attitude and choice as it relates to this creative force which moves with absolute certainty in the affairs of the world at this time. It may be said that there never was a time when it wasn't moving, but there is a particular period of climax in which we now find ourselves when, as it was put somewhere in the Bible, time should be no more. That statement can be interpreted in various ways but it does indicate that the interlude of human self-centeredness, the interlude of non-man, comes to an end. We find ourselves associated with a greater understanding of what is occurring in this regard in our own experience and in our own realm of responsibility.

If, seeing these things, we are to play an intelligent part in what is occurring, so that we do not find ourselves in conflict with it, we must recognize that what is called love is the key. Love is a creative force. We need to allow our understanding of this reality to be lifted out of the human view of things, the limited sentimental view of what is spoken of as love, in order to become aware increasingly of what the truth is, the truth of love; for here is the very core of the irresistible creative force which moves throughout the whole cosmos in the achievement of the natural purposes of God.

We have recognized love as the name given to one of the four creative forces, which in turn are the differentiations of the one irresistible force which proceeds from God to operate in the realm of space and time where we have our place of experience. In the world of space and time this one irresistible force, this one river, divides into four heads, which we have called the four forces and designated by specific names. The names, obviously, are not the forces but they do give some indication of the particular nature of the respective forces. All forces are in operation all the time; the irresistible force never stops being irresistible; but there is a sequence of dominance in the creative cycle. That sequence places the names of the four forces in a certain order: water, air, earth and fire.

Fire has been used as a symbol of love. There are other such symbols; each of them indicates certain aspects of the nature of this creative force. Fire particularly portrays the working of this force in transmuting substance into spirit. We may see a rather apt symbol in fire. By the way, *fire* is a word, a word-symbol, which describes a process, a process which in our present consideration is also a symbol. So the word *fire* is a symbol of a symbol; the actuality of the process is the symbol of a certain aspect of the operation of the creative force of love. Love transmutes.

We might note in the symbol of fire certain factors which convey an increased understanding of the nature of love. If, for instance, there is a candle burning, solid substance is being transmuted into gaseous substance. We see here a change taking place which well symbolizes the transmutation of physical substance into the substance of spirit. Gas, or air, is the symbol of spirit. The evidence of that transmutation is seen in the flame. The flame includes various colors, principally yellow and blue. The blue is at the core, the yellow is on the periphery. Of course, actually, the whole spectrum is here. But the yellow part of the flame is hot and if we unwisely put a finger into it it's painful; we get burned. However, the blue part of the flame is cool and if by some means you can get in there you will not be burned. The yellow flame will be all around you and that will be hot, but in the core of the flame it is cool.

This symbolizes rather well the place where man belongs. He belongs at the core of the flame and in that position he doesn't get burned, but moving out from that position into what is symbolized by the yellow part of the flame he finds it to be a painful and disturbing business. Evidently, then, man has been out of place. Of course, man out of place is no longer man. Man is man only when he is in place; then he is what was described as a 'living soul'. When he gets out of place he finds himself in the hot part of the flame; he gets burned and eventually reduced to ashes. They say in the funeral service, 'Dust to dust, ashes to ashes.' But in the process of being burned he finds himself in pain, in a realm of suffering, in a realm of considerable disturbance.

Now, there is nothing wrong with the yellow part of the flame, any more than there is anything wrong with the blue part of the flame. There is nothing wrong with the burning process when it is rightly under control. Here again we can see in the symbol of fire indication of two possibilities. Fire is a force. It is a force which may create destruction, or if it is rightly under control, even in the realm of self-centered human function, it is found to be useful and of a seemingly constructive nature. Fire is the symbol of love. As long as this irresistible force is finding release according to its true nature, which is controlled, it is constructive throughout the universe; but when human beings resist that irresistible force it becomes destructive in their own experience because in that realm it is removed from its true nature and the natural control is lost. It is lost in the experience of human beings; it isn't lost from the standpoint of the working of this irresistible force, because the truth of love cannot possibly be separated from itself. It is itself, and it is the nature of love to reveal itself.

Love and truth, the truth of love – love and truth are inseparable in fact. They seem to become parted in the consciousness of human beings and in their experience, but what has happened? Human experience has moved from the core of the flame into the periphery of the flame. The periphery of the flame relates to the transmutation process, the process where change is occurring. Change occurs easily and naturally by reason of the working of the creative force of love, but when human self-consciousness moves into that realm pain is experienced. Human self-consciousness has become mixed with the substance which is to be changed. The changing process is not meant to be contained in the self-consciousness of human beings and it is not so when human identity is restored to the state of the living soul at the cool center of the flame. Then, whatever transmutation needs to occur on the periphery can do so without producing tribulation – tribulation in the consciousness of man. The change continues to occur; the burning process, the transmutation process, goes on, rightly so; but human beings should not be involved in it. Man is not identified with the changes that are occurring; he is, on the contrary, identified with the force which is producing the changes.

The restoration of man brings his self-consciousness back into the place where man is a living soul. In that position 'the former things are passed away'. There is no more pain, no more sorrow or crying, no more death – because death relates to this transmutation process, the place where man does not belong. Returning to the place where he does belong he experiences the state of the living soul and from that position he is capable of observing what occurs in the transmutation realm. But no longer being involved with it, it is not painful to him; it is, rather, a delight to him. We have a play on words here, don't we? — de-light, or the light. It is a light, a joy to him. The outer part of the flame gives light, doesn't it? This presumably was the reason for lighting a candle, so that we might be able to see at night. But the light comes from the outer part of the flame, not from the core of the flame. The light of the flame is the evidence that the core is present. There would be no light on the periphery of the flame if there were not the core of the flame, because the transmutation process proceeds from the core. The force of transmutation emerges at the center of things, and the center of things is where man belongs.

There has been a TV program in Canada called *Man at the Center*; I do not know whether it still continues. It was rather a meaningless program but the statement was true; man belongs at the center, but as man, a living soul. He becomes that living soul, he is restored to the center of things, through love, by reason of the truth of love. Love is the key.

Human experience of love has heretofore related man almost entirely to what is external to himself. He loves externals, whether those externals are other human beings or things in general. His love of externals has established an attitude of like and dislike, and fundamentally it is like and dislike that govern human function. What governs human function may be described as god. So human likes and dislikes have constituted the character, the nature, of the god which he worships, the god which controls his existence, such as it is, in the flame, in the periphery of the flame — because this is a false god which has removed him from his place at the core. It has dragged him out from the core into the realm where the transmutation is occurring.

The transmutation should be occurring; there is nothing wrong with that. The only thing wrong is that man, with his self-consciousness, is present in that realm; and that's something he doesn't like, so he tries in various ways to mitigate his unhappy lot. He tries in various ways to devise methods of pleasing himself, of entertaining himself, of reducing his suffering. He is so accustomed to the experience of suffering that it only becomes really impressive when it is greatly increased. He lives in a state of suffering. This is why there is so much unhappiness, so much complaint, so much that isn't liked. So it has come to the pass that if the suffering can be reduced somewhat, if he can be distracted from it for a little while, he considers that that is happiness, that is joy, that is something just wonderful. But it isn't the true experience at all; it merely is a slight contrast to the misery which is constantly present. Reduce the misery because by some means you are able to forget it for a moment and thereby, it is imagined, one has been released into a happy experience. We have such states obviously present in the drunk, or in the person who is subject to hallucinating drugs, or whatever. Just for a moment, the misery is obscured, damped, and it seems so wonderful; but it is all part of the same experience. If we can deaden that experience somewhat, then that seems tremendous. We were suffering so before and now the suffering's gone! Take two aspirins and go to bed! If we can anesthetize the misery, then that's supposed to be happiness; and human beings have been thoroughly fooled on this score.

But there is no real experience of what happiness is anywhere but in the core where man belongs. It can't be experienced on the periphery. The periphery is the place where, if man takes his consciousness, it is going to be painful. So instead of trying to find ways and means of anesthetizing ourselves from the pain, how much more intelligent it would be to consider possibilities of returning to the core where the pain isn't. The only way by which there may be such a return is through the key of love. If we love and are governed by our likes and dislikes, we're trapped – we're trapped on the periphery of the flame and we get burned, eventually so badly burned that what we thought ourselves to be is reduced to ashes. And that's part of the transmutation process; there's nothing wrong with that. But we may, if we will, love in another way.

It is said that the Lord God formed man in the beginning, formed him of the dust of the ground, and breathed into his nostrils the breath of life so that man became a living soul. Here is the true state of man at the core, at the place where the Lord God emerges into the realm of space and time. Obviously, for this emergence to occur, the means would necessarily be made in the image and likeness of what was to emerge; the means would be created in the shape, we might say, of what was to appear by reason of the emergence of the Lord God. So man belongs at that core point, at the crossover point out of the realm which from the standpoint of a consciousness of space and time does not exist, out of the realm of nowhere, into the realm of now here.

We return to the place where we belong as man, male and female, because we love the Lord God. The words *Lord God* describe the truth of being for man. Particularly they describe the truth of being for man collectively, for the whole of mankind in other words. But the same truth, in principle, applies to the individual. The Lord God in the individual sense may be indicated by using other words perhaps. 'The angel of the Lord' is one form of terminology which has been used to describe the truth of the being of man, the truth of man which is known at the core. It cannot be known anywhere else.

It is useless for man to stay out in the yellow part of the flame and look toward the core, trying to figure out what the core is, suffering the while. This is what most of religious function in human beings has been – we're sinners and we stay out in the flame; we burn. We confess our sins but that doesn't seem to do much good; we still stay out in the flame, and we hopefully look toward the core. But we see nothing. It is like looking up into the sky, isn't it, during the day. On a clear day we see nothing but blue. There is something up there, which we discover at night, but during the day, in the heat of the sun, when we look into the sky we see nothing but blue. And when we stand out in the periphery of the flame and look toward the core we see nothing but blue; we see nothing, in other words.

But if the human capacity to love is turned toward the Lord God instead of toward what is external to us, then we find ourselves moving in the creative cycle, being drawn back into place, being restored to the core where we belong. To love the Lord God is to love the truth of our own being, the real quality of our own nature. As we open ourselves in love in that direction we begin to become more conscious, consequently, of what our true nature is. But every time our love swings us around to involve us with our likes and dislikes in the external sense, we descend into the realm where the painful trans-mutation is taking place – painful insofar as we are concerned.

The first great commandment was to love the Lord thy God with all. We see how sensible this is, but we are not trying to love something that to us doesn't exist. This is the effort that most human beings put forth when they turn toward what they call God, because to them God does not really exist; He is nowhere. We must turn toward something that is now here, turn toward the quality and the evidence of the quality and nature of the Lord God, the evidence of the quality and nature of man – of man, the living soul. Human being are thoroughly hung up on non-man, the dying soul; and wherever human beings look in the external sense they see non-man. And this non-man they like and that non-man they dislike. All this traps human beings in the flame. The moth comes to the flame, doesn't it, the brightness of the flame, and it gets burned. Human beings think they see the realm where it is going to be so bright and glorious, the realm around them in the environment. After all, some may say, this is where the garden of God should be, this is where heaven on earth should be. True enough, but how does it appear? Through man, not through non-man, and as long as non-man is predominant and human beings look at each other and worship each other it cannot appear. This business of falling in love that we have talked about is often described as one person worshiping another, isn't it? We have no business worshiping each other, non-people, but we love the Lord our God, we love the truth of ourselves, the truth of what we are, the truth of man the living soul, which is the Lord God.

As we begin to become aware of this nature and this becomes supremely important to us because of our love for it, then our total concern is to permit this nature to extend beyond us. We find ourselves in place and this nature extending beyond us. And what is that nature? It is the irresistible force. We begin to find ourselves a part of what may be described as the immovable mass, which to human beings is nowhere but to man is now here because man is now here. And when man, the living soul, is now here, what proceeds from him is the irresistible force. The core aspect of that irresistible force relates to what we call love, and it is through this movement of the irresistible force in its controlled creative cycles that the transmutation takes place correctly in the environment and in our own physical bodies which are a part of the environment. Changes come in the flesh. All things are made new.

Here we can begin to see, to understand, and to experience these things – no longer hidden behind the fog but beginning to emerge into the realm of our awareness and experience, which is what occurs on the fourth day of creation, during the dominant movement of the fourth force. The mists clear and the reality of being, the truth of being, emerges into awareness and experience and becomes dominant to us. The hold that likes and dislikes have had over us begins to recede and the governing control, dominion, of the truth of our own being emerges. What a glorious experience this is! We stand where we belong once again, and while for the time being there may be a consciousness of the turmoil and of the pain – maybe in our own physical bodies and around us everywhere – we are no longer dominated by that. We are no longer controlled by that, because our concern is simply to express the truth of love, the truth of our own being. There is then round about us the flame; we stand in the midst of the flame; that is, the yellow part of the flame is all around us.

The transmutation is occurring all around us – the transmutation which is primarily taking place in the consciousness of human beings, in the de-structuring of the human consciousness. The structured forms are burned. The substance composing those structured forms is transmuted into spirit – a quality of substance within the scope of this world of space and time which may then take form according to the design inherent in the irresistible force, spiritual form. In that spiritual form we find a living expression, not a dead and disintegrating expression. The structured human consciousness is dead and in the process of disintegration under the influence of the flame. But when the flame is allowed to intensify, the furnace heated seven times hotter than it's wont to be heated, the structured consciousness very quickly is dissolved and what corresponds to the gases is released, and gas easily takes form in whatever the vessel of manifestation may be.

When that vessel is provided by the irresistible force, then what appears in consciousness is true to the truth. Because it appears in the consciousness of man it begins to take form around man in the physical sense, in the external sense. The garden is restored, the beauty of the earth comes again as it is designed to be, because of the presence of man. Here is our responsibility, of which we begin to become increasingly aware so that we may assume the proper attitude, in openness of heart to the truth of our own being, that this may emerge and all that is contrary to that truth may be dissolved in the heat of the fire of God's love.

The Perfect, the Upright and the Beautiful

'Immediately after the tribulation of those days shall the sun be darkened, and the moon shall not give her light, and the stars shall fall from heaven, and the powers of the heavens shall be shaken:

'And then shall appear the sign of the Son of man in heaven: and then shall all the tribes of the earth mourn, and they shall see the Son of man coming in the clouds of heaven with power and great glory.

'And he shall send his angels with a great sound of a trumpet, and they shall gather together his elect from the four winds, from one end of heaven to the other.'

It is said that coming events cast their shadows before, and this is always true. What is here spoken of as tribulation, a tribulation previously indicated to be more than had ever been experienced by human beings on earth, is yet to come. We see a shadow in this regard being cast before. By the same token, the shadow of what occurs after the tribulation is also cast before. Nothing ever happens without warning. Many people might be inclined to dispute that statement but it nevertheless is the fact. Certainly warnings are frequently overlooked or not noticed, but coming events do cast their shadows before.

As we have before noted, everything moves in cycles. When a particular cycle comes to the point of culmination there may be very rapid movement, so that it seems from certain standpoints to be instantaneous. But to reach that point where it seems that way there was all that was involved in the previous part of the cycle. The previous part was not moving as rapidly as it seems at the time of climax, but the movement was there nevertheless. It is important that one should perceive such movement before it comes to the point where the experience is extremely rapid. If one has one's back turned until that point is reached, one is going to be taken by surprise and is not going to be able to handle what occurs. There is a need to be ahead of the game, so to speak, so that whatever may put in an appearance can be handled easily in the right way.

There are many evidences of the tribulation to come. There are also evidences within the range of our awareness of what it is that comes after the tribulation. In fact, we recognize two aspects of one cycle here. There is that which is passing away and there is that which is taking form; there is disintegration and there is integration, and both these aspects of the one cycle give evidence of their coming.

Because human beings are so very much involved with externals, the aspect of impending tribulation emphasizes itself in consciousness the most, and while the nature of the troubles which are yet to come may not be seen clearly for what they will be, nevertheless there is this sense of impending doom in the awareness of many people. There are, of course, the so-called prophets of doom, and others who seek to discount their prophecy. There can be arguments this way and that; nevertheless coming events do cast their shadows before.

Our concern, of course, is not so much with the tribulation, although there is the obvious need to be in position to handle it, but rather with what emerges because of the falling away of the first heaven and the first earth to reveal the new heaven and the new earth. Our concern is with the latter. The former is an incidental necessity, so there is no need to look upon it with fear or to see it as doom. It only appears to be doom if what is presently the state is thought of as being worth saving. The first heaven and the first earth properly pass away, and if they give evidence of their passing in a more worldwide sense, then that is rightly cause for thanksgiving.

The first heaven and the first earth, the present human condition, is seen sometimes as being good, more often as being bad. Last night on the TV there was a showing of a 1967 film entitled *The Good, the Bad and the Ugly*. Some of you may have seen it, or have seen it before, and while I do not think that the presentation was particularly edifying, it nevertheless does portray rather graphically the human condition. This is supposed to be one of the better moving pictures and is accepted as entertainment, presumably because people feel a certain sense of relatedness to what is portrayed. If a portrayal doesn't provide something that relates in human consciousness to the people who observe, then it isn't considered to be fitting entertainment.

But here, certainly symbolically at least, was a portrayal of what is present in people: good, bad and ugly. Insofar as the good was concerned, there were momentary evidences of compassion on the part of the one who portrayed that aspect of the trinity; the bad was unrelievedly bad; and the ugly was ugly but at the same time rather pathetic. Human beings have in their own makeup the good and the bad in this present human condition of the first heaven and the first earth; the result of this is ugly, ugliness. This fact is not always seen as being so, but it is so and would be so seen if there were a real consciousness of the true condition of man, the condition of the new heaven and the new earth. That state could be described as the perfect, the upright and the beautiful. If it were possible for human beings to make a moving picture along these lines, I doubt if it would be considered entertainment by most. Why? Because there would be so precious little sense of relatedness to it. The good, the bad and the ugly are paramount. Nevertheless, while this may be human experience at the present time, the truth of man is otherwise. The truth of man, we have come to recognize, is the angel, who is perfect and upright and beautiful.

The tribulation occurs because of the degraded quality of human experience bringing its inevitable results. We see this shadow darkening the sky. It is said that it is always darkest just before the dawn. Whether that is actually true or not, I wouldn't say; but it is true in the sense of human experience and is true with respect to what is occurring in the world in these latter days. The darkness of tribulation intensifies, but at the same time the dawn is at hand. The new heaven and the new earth are present, as they always have been, but the time when that condition in the experience of human beings may be known is closely associated with the intensifying darkness of tribulation.

Recently we were considering what has been unfolding in India and other countries in that vicinity. It has seemed that those people have a certain spiritual quality more definitely emphasized than in what might be called the Western world. In the Western world the ability to achieve has been particularly developed and there has been the idea that material gain, wealth and physical satisfaction were the road to fulfilment. A certain success in following this road has been known, so that most of those who have been involved in this state have been thoroughly occupied with material things. This has brought to many a seeming prosperity which has seemed good, desirable. On the other hand, in a country like India, where there are over half a billion people in an area considerably smaller than the United States, or Canada for that matter, while there has been a limited evidence of material wealth, the population in the overall sense has been extremely poor and the conditions of life have been hard and painful. But because there seemed no particular expectation of alleviation in this regard, attention was turned more to what might be classified as spiritual things in order that some sort of satisfaction might be experienced in that sense. But whether the pendulum has swung in that direction, insofar as those people are concerned, or in the other direction insofar as the people of the Western world are concerned, it has all been a part of the good, the bad and the ugly, all a part of the first heaven and the first earth.

In all the areas of the world, with all the peoples of the world, there has been the development of trappings of various sorts with which those concerned have been most thoroughly preoccupied. Whether those trappings were classified as being spiritual or material made precious little difference. There are what are called religions in the world supposed to be spiritual. These religions are characterized by trappings of all kinds. Christianity is quite outstanding in this regard, but the same is true of the Hindus or the Buddhists or the Moslems, or whoever. There are the trappings in the realm that was supposed to be spiritual, and of course there are the trappings in the realm which is obviously material – all of it a cover-up of the truth, of the angel.

It is indicated that after the tribulation the sign of the Son of man would be seen in heaven and the Son of man would come 'in the clouds of heaven with power and great glory.' This is one of the passages in the Bible which have been taken and developed to indicate what human beings imagine the second coming of Christ would be. If these were our Master's words, He certainly did refer to Himself on many occasions, evidently, as the 'Son of man', but who has really known who He was or who He is? He has been covered with the trappings of what has been called Christianity, so that the truth was almost entirely obscured. But there is the truth nevertheless. Perhaps we have had the opportunity of glimpsing something of that truth.

One of the evidences of His coming – whatever that would mean; let us not speculate in this regard – is that He sends His angels to gather the elect. And coming events cast their shadows before. Are we to suppose that the angels that are sent are discarnate spiritual beings of some kind who will move around on the face of the earth tapping the elect on the shoulder, saying, 'Come with me'? No, we by our own experience have become aware in some measure that the angel is incarnate in human form but only has opportunity to act on earth when the human form cooperates, when the human form, with its consciousness, is willing to let the angel come, so that there is the evidence of the angel on earth.

This, of course, is exactly what occurred insofar as the man Jesus was concerned. The particular angel involved was indeed rather special – insofar as this world is concerned could not have been more special, an archangel indeed, one who may rightly be referred to as the Lord, the Supreme One. When He was on earth, manifesting in human form, in fact made evident in human form, precious few at the time were aware of it. Even those who were closest to Him didn't really comprehend it. Subsequently others have looked back and thought they understood, but no one really understands except in the experience of the present moment. Those people who lived at the time of Jesus had the opportunity of understanding because that was the present moment for them. That they didn't understand, that they didn't really see, that they were not aware of what was happening, is perhaps a sad commentary on human beings; but it also indicates that those who have lived since have been in the same sort of darkness, because all they have been able to see – or think they see – is something in imagination, which no doubt they try to believe most earnestly, but it's still imagination. The people concerned were not there when it actually happened, and it is quite evident that if they had been they would have had no more awareness than those who were there. It is self-righteous arrogance for anyone to presume anything else until or unless the opportunity is available and accepted in the present moment for a similar experience in principle. Then, if they know it now, it might be inferred that they would also have known it then; but that is the only valid ground upon which a person may stand if he is to emerge out of this self-righteous state of arrogance – at least in what is called the Christian world. There are those who believe, or try to, on this imaginary Jesus, and there are those who disbelieve this imaginary Jesus. Is one really better than the other, do you think? All of them may be classified as the good, the bad and the ugly.

When the angels are sent forth into the earth to gather the elect, those angels are made evident in human form. The elect are those human beings who, touching the radiance of the angel in whatever way, awaken, perhaps without understanding, to the truth of what is present. This awakening has been occurring in some measure in many places and there are those who touch something, sense it, but in varying degrees still observe through their trappings. From the standpoint of the angel, or the angels, there is love for angels; there is no love for the trappings. However, most people love their trappings; to this extent they are unable to love the angel when he appears, just as those who were on earth in the vicinity of our Master long ago were unable to love Him to the extent that they were involved with their trappings. Human beings, because they love their trappings, insulate themselves from the angels who are sent. Only to the degree that they relinquish their trappings will they let themselves be gathered together.

This is why the angels are sent, isn't it? – to gather the elect from the four winds, from one end of the heaven to the other. The heaven relates to something of consciousness, as the earth relates to something of physical form. We have spoken of our ministry as being a vibrational ministry, relating to the realm of consciousness. The gathering takes place in the heaven. The angels are sent to gather the elect from one end of the heaven to the other. There is just one heaven, even though there is a great variety of trappings in relationship to that heaven. Human consciousness is thoroughly embedded in these structures which imprison people in the present human condition. But the angel, coming on earth through human form, has the responsibility of gathering the elect, those who are willing, who elect to be gathered. The gathering of the elect permits the increased evidence of angels on earth because the human forms concerned, leaving behind their trappings, become the facility for the angelic expression.

So we see here a portrayal in this way of the angelic ministry, the true purpose of the angel on earth at this present time: to gather the elect from the four winds – four quarters make a whole – out of all mankind, from one end of the heaven to the other, so that there may be the expanding facility for the angelic expression on earth. It is through this that the purposes of God are served.

Angels love angels, so the concern is to provide what is necessary to permit angels to be made evident on earth in human form. There may be compassion insofar as humans are concerned. It is said that 'God so loved the world,' and this is taken to mean that He loved human beings. No. He loves His own. He does not love whatever obscures His own; He does not love the trappings, whether they be of Christianity, of Islam, of Hinduism, Buddhism, or any other of the trappings on the face of the earth in the religious sense. Neither does He love the trappings in the sense of human ideologies and cultures. He loves the incarnate angels but He has no use for what obscures the incarnate angels. The prince of this world is lost. The Lord is not interested in trying to save the prince of this world; He is not interested in trying to save the human trappings; He is not interested in trying to save humans who determine to involve themselves with those trappings. The true attitude of love says, in effect, to hell with them – to the fire, that all may be consumed. If the fire burns increasingly it is because of the real nature of God's love. If there is tribulation, that is evidence of the burning; that is evidence of the true nature of love. It isn't an evil thing in the sense of something which shouldn't be; it is part of the essential process by which nothing but the angelic expression may remain on earth.

Those who are the angels of the Lord have this attitude. While they are deeply concerned for other angels and for the increase of the angelic expression wherever it may appear, so that they handle the unreal trappings with care, that care is not because there is any love for the trappings but because there is love for the angel. I love you as angels. I have no use for the trappings which may remain in you or in me; they are valueless and meaningless. They are nauseating; and while one is willing to be in a nauseating circumstance because an angel may be there, that does not make the circumstance any less nauseating. The trappings are always so to an angel of the Lord. He may be under the necessity of dealing with those trappings as they appear in relationship to somebody else. That somebody else, in his eyes, is the angel of the Lord, who is just as nauseated by the trappings as you are. So, disposing of the trappings is a most needed requirement in our serving, and sometimes the only way that the trappings can be disposed of is for them to depart with those who identify themselves as workers of iniquity.

The good, the bad and the ugly – let them pass away! Do not hold on to them because you find a relatedness to them in yourself. Just because you have a relatedness to such things in yourself does not mean that you have to associate yourself with them in another. Let them pass away. The angel will not pass away in any case, although under that circumstance it may be that he will pass for the moment from your range of association. The world is being cleansed. Let us be associated with the means by which this happens, rather than with what is being cleansed away. We do not serve anyone by maintaining association with the false trappings just because we have some false trappings in ourselves that coordinate with those in someone else. When you have the angel consciousness false trappings anywhere will be nauseating to you and you will not get very close to the trappings. The only concern is to be close to the angel. If the trappings insist upon intervening between the angel and you, then what is there to be done? Just simply let the trappings pass away and they will pass away from you. The angel will not, but there will be no particular evidence that this is so for the moment specifically in that instance, because the angel, under necessity, stays with those trappings until they have experienced the second death.

So, as angels we are responsible for gathering the elect from the four winds, from one end of the heaven to the other. Gathering the elect implies gathering those human bodies and minds which are willing to be gathered to us because we stand as angels on earth.

True Consciousness Restored

We come to the point of an awareness that changes are necessary, changes which primarily occur in consciousness. We need to see that we do have a responsibility in this matter.

Now, we might recognize that the changes which are to occur are of such a nature as to allow the experience of something in living entirely different from what is commonly known on earth in the world now. If we talk about changes, we're not really talking about adjustments so that we might somehow or other become better people perhaps, whatever that would be. There is a state of consciousness on earth that is a false condition, and by reason of this state of consciousness we have a state of affairs around us which is false, distorted, destructive, and leading toward disaster. The changes which are to occur are not going to be achieved by some effort on our own part from the standpoint of our conscious minds. The usual view is that all we need to do is to undertake to do some thinking about what's going on and then, having thought, we will be in a position to make things different. Perhaps this rather relates to the psychological, or the psychiatric approach even, where it is supposed that we can figure it all out and determine how things should be, and then merely apply what we think we understand to the experience of life. But the fundamental premise that is present in our consciousness now is a false premise, and if we start from this false premise we end up with something false. There is the necessity of change produced by something other than the conscious mind of man, the educated intellect, because fundamentally it is this 'exalted intelligence' that has produced the appalling state of affairs that we find on earth.

We might pause to consider for a moment the fact that there are various levels of consciousness within the scope of our own experience. The conscious mind we could define by using the term 'surface consciousness'. The surface consciousness is actually a rather thin layer on top of what is subsurface. Now the subsurface consciousness occupies far greater volume than the surface layer of consciousness with which we think we think. This surface layer is governed very largely by what is immediately subsurface. What erupts from the subsurface levels of consciousness tends to control, to govern, to determine, how we think at the surface. Of course, at the surface we are very ingenious in explaining and rationalizing the intelligence of what we do, when in fact what we do is almost entirely based upon what has erupted from the subsurface levels of consciousness.

Now, there is a mess subsurface and there is a mess on the surface. I suppose this might be compared a little bit to the ocean when there are waves, sometimes maybe a forty-foot wave, but if you go subsurface you don't have to go very far down actually before there is no evidence of what is occurring on the surface. There is a calmness below. This provides something of an analogy in relationship to what is true of our own experience of consciousness. We have a surface consciousness which is very much aware of the waves and the wind, and human beings are rather easily disturbed. Below the level of that surface there is a continuing disturbance to a certain depth, but below that depth we begin to come into another area, which I suppose might be referred to as subocean or subterranean or something – deeper, anyway, than the immediately subsurface – and in this area we begin to penetrate to a level of consciousness through which many things work but of which we are completely oblivious. What is working through there, amongst other things, makes it possible for us to be alive. A certain control is in operation with respect to our physical bodies, of course, and the body is coordinated after a fashion by whatever it is that is working through these deeper levels of the subsurface consciousness. Now, what is working through those levels produces and maintains life; it also produces and maintains the higher levels of the subsurface consciousness and the surface consciousness. If we weren't alive we wouldn't have any of that.

Now, if we look at other forms of life here on earth other than human we find that there are present subsurface levels of consciousness in all these forms, maybe not reaching to the higher levels as are present in the human sense, but nevertheless there are sub-surface levels of consciousness in plants and animals that are similar to what is present in ourselves. By reason of these subsurface levels of consciousness there is the evidence of life in the vegetable kingdom and in the animal kingdom and in the human kingdom. Something is able to work at these levels to produce what we know and call life. We can't somehow isolate that life and find out what it is; we merely know that it's a fact; we have the experience. And we don't need a very intelligent intellect to inform us that we have that experience, do we? We just have the experience; we're alive. And the bird flying around is alive — it doesn't have to figure it out; it just knows the fact. So there is something that has been operating in the deeper levels of the subsurface consciousness which has allowed us to continue on earth in spite of the disturbances that are present closer to the surface and in spite of what has been going on at the surface.

Now this surface consciousness, as we see, is very much the result of what is occurring immediately subsurface, and what is occurring immediately subsurface relates to the various experiences that we've had during the course of our existence here on earth thus far and also reaches back into the past, into the hereditary past, so that there are many things in this subsurface layer that have come down to us from our forebears. And all these things exert influence, and all these things condition what occurs at the surface. At the surface we are inclined to think we are free agents and that we can think things out and think things through and determine how we should act and all this. But we begin to see, if we recognize these principles, that in fact we are puppets governed by what is going on subsurface and which emerges at the surface level. And emerging at the surface level, think-ing of ourselves as free agents, we behave in a manner which seeks to take control of our actions; but really our actions are being deter-mined by what is immediately subsurface, which has come out of the world around us — the influences which have impinged upon us — and out of the hereditary past. Now, this is what is called a human being now, but it is in fact a far cry from what should be; it is a false state of affairs.

However, there is something which is true about us, otherwise we wouldn't even be alive. There is something working at the deeper levels of this subsurface consciousness which has operated to produce our physical bodies – from a single cell, mind you. Impossible, isn't it? – a miracle. People take it for granted, but what a marvelous thing. Here is something at work which was quite capable of building this intricate organism and of generating the capacity of consciousness in it in its various levels all the way up to the surface level. Could it be that there is something above the surface as well? Human beings are earthbound. Nowadays we are able to make machines which take us up into the air, move us around, but left to our own devices we have to plod along on the earth, right on the surface. But there is something above, in the planetary sense. We are, in fact, when we're walking on the surface of the planet, at the bottom of the envelope of air. There is air above us.

Human experience tends to grub around in the dirt, doesn't it, on the surface of the earth. We're all involved with everything that's going on around here and behaving on the basis of what we observe and of the influences that come to us out of the environment, and of the influences that emerge from the subsurface levels of our consciousness out of the hereditary past. And so we tend to be limited to a rather thin layer here on the surface of the earth and on the surface of our life experience as individuals. Now, if there has been a force, a power, at work through the subsurface levels of consciousness, the deeper layers, which has been capable of producing what has been produced, causing us to be individuals with the capacity of consciousness at all its various levels, would it not seem to be reasonable that this same power could keep moving through the subsurface layers, eventually to emerge at the surface, so that the control which is present at the deeper levels of consciousness might begin to be experienced in the levels of consciousness that are immediately subsurface and then through that at the level of the surface consciousness? But, of course, what has happened is that with our surface consciousness, under the influences that are present, which we have noted, we tend to try to take charge of things and make the world behave the way we want it to behave.

Now, in man alone is there this surface level of consciousness. All other forms of life, we may say, are limited to the subsurface, and all other forms of life then tend to know a greater control of this power working through them, and we find what is called instinct. Of course, human beings have messed things up a good deal and distorted this pattern considerably, but, left to its own devices, nature has a way of balancing out; in other words, the controls are operating there. Only where this surface level of human consciousness gets in is there a messing up of the pattern.

Now, we may recognize that there is something above this surface level; I suppose we could call it supersurface. Subsurface, surface and supersurface. But if we get stuck at the surface and we think this is fine – now we're sentient beings; now we're able to be very intelligent, to do such intelligent things and produce such wonderful progress in our civilization here on earth, and all this – then we just stay grubbing around at the surface and we have no awareness of the fact that there is anything supersurface. What was emerging from the deeper levels of the subsurface, pure and clear, establishing a right control in the physical form, etc., producing the levels of further consciousness, is blocked by reason of what is immediately subsurface and at the surface. It can't come all the way through. It keeps us alive for a little while but that's all. And anyone who is really honest knows that there should be a greater experience than what comes. Human beings feel inadequate in various ways, frustrated, etc. That's the way they should feel, because they are blocking the very thing which would allow the full experience which would lead into the supersurface experience.

Now, the changes that are required are not so much at the surface at the moment as those changes which are essential to clear the subsurface pattern, so that what is in the deeper layers may come up without distortion through the immediately subsurface layers to the surface layer. And, emerging at the surface layer, a person says, 'Oh, I see, I understand.' Now, I can speak to you who are gathered here this evening along these lines and I trust that many of you are in position to say, 'Oh, I see, I understand,' whereas one could have a gathering of people in a general sense in the world and speak of these things and it would be nonsense, wouldn't mean anything, because there was nothing yet filtering through, so to speak, to reach the surface layer of consciousness. Now, there is a working of this – what will we call it? – life force (actually it may be accurately defined as the spirit of God) working in the deeper levels of the subsurface layers of consciousness. It is working down there but it is also working at the same time from above. In other words, there is a penetration from above through the supersurface levels of consciousness – from below and from above. And the surface layer is the connecting link between the two. I suppose it could be compared to the fact that there is the sun shining down through the atmosphere to the surface of the earth, as well as something happening in the earth which allows things to grow, which allows the various forms of life to rise up, composed of the substance of the earth. So there is something working from below and there's something working from above, and this is true in our own situation.

In order to begin to experience what is present supersurface there must be the essential changes working out subsurface, that that which is rising up from below may clarify the surface level of consciousness to the point where it can experience what is supersurface. As long as we're all involved in this distortion which is subsurface, that's all it sees, that's all it understands. And it's a mess. It may be a factual state of affairs in the experience of the person but it's not really the truth of the matter, because it's not really the way the person should be. There should be a clarity all the way through, to all the levels of consciousness. Now, in order for that to come, the changes must work out subsurface, and those changes are not going to come by anything that the surface level of consciousness can do, which, I suppose, is most disappointing to those who are intellectually inclined. But their intellectual achievements tend to do them no good, tend to accomplish nothing, because what needs to happen is for the spirit of God, this life force which is working at the lower levels of subsurface consciousness, to be allowed to move up into the higher levels of that same consciousness, to clear and sort out and correctly polarize what is there present. And as this happens, then finally it comes through to the surface level of consciousness and the individual begins to consciously understand.

Now, a conscious understanding doesn't come through what are deemed to be educational processes, according to the present idea of human beings. It comes by reason of something over which human beings have no control whatsoever but to which there may be a yielding, a willingness to allow what is moving in the deeper levels of the subsurface consciousness to do what needs to be done. Now, this is usually looked upon in religious circles as something more or less haphazard. The outpouring of the spirit may come, usually down through the ceiling somehow, to transform the person, and there's no assurance about it; if God feels like it today He will release a little, or hold back, or whatever. But, in fact, there's no holding back at any time. The provision is here; the fact of it is in our experience of being alive. It is working, but constantly being blocked by the surface level, which maintains disturbance in the subsurface level because we are constantly finding ourselves reacting to what is experienced out of the environment or what is experienced coming from the hereditary pattern in our subsurface level of consciousness. And so there is a reflection back and forth. Something rises up out of the subsurface level, hits the surface level and bounces back again. And so it's all maintained in this disturbed state.

Now there is something that the conscious, surface level needs to do, but the conscious surface level is not required to try to reeducate the subsurface levels, because it doesn't know, it doesn't know what should be. It has no faintest idea, and it can't possibly find out what it is through reading books. If what I say to you has value to you it's not because I am merely conveying some information to the surface level of your consciousness; it is because something is being offered from a supersurface standpoint and also from a subsurface standpoint. In other words, there's something coming down from above and there's something coming up from below, and if your surface consciousness will stay still in the middle, then something can happen. If the surface consciousness tries to grasp what it is that is being said it will go off into ideas over here and into ideas over there – and this means that, and that means the other thing – and it will be in a thorough whirl. But if it's willing just to stay still, to enjoy the momentary experience, whatever it is, without trying to figure it out, then there is something at work from above and from below. Now, the whole exercise, one might say, from the conscious standpoint is just to be still. This is too much to ask of most surface consciousnesses, because they're in a whirl most of the time, usually about all the things that they don't think they understand. Oh, that would be confusion, wouldn't it, because they don't understand anything, really; so it's not surprising if they may feel they don't understand. OK, what's the difference? Just stay still in the middle and, recognizing the fact that there is something working subsurface in each person, and recognizing the fact that, in a situation such as this, I may provide something supersurface, then the twain can begin to meet and something actually happens. Surely we're interested in something happening. Lots of people attend meetings and lectures and listen to this and listen to that, and examine into this and examine into that, imagining that thereby they are getting somewhere; but nothing really happens, because there's no change in the fundamental quality and nature of consciousness. The individual retains the previous state. It's still there – no change.

By reason of the working of this creative force – the spirit of God, life force, whatever it might be called – the changes are wrought. This is how it's done. This is moving constantly, as long as life remains. When we stop blocking its movement by our ridiculous antics in the surface and immediately subsurface layers of consciousness, something may begin to come through. Now, most of what is required in human experience, in the general sense, relates to subsurface layers of consciousness. It isn't more supposed intellectual brilliance; it's that something should actually happen creatively below the surface level of consciousness, and it is not going to happen by anything that the intellect can do. If it happens, the experience of the intellect will change and the individual will find himself being released from a self experience that has been merely human to an experience of the truth of his own being. That experience is known in the supersurface levels of consciousness. That's where we belong: caught up into the air, so to speak. I think Paul said something about that in the Bible. Whether he knew what he was talking about or not, I don't know – whether he saw the truth of the matter or whether he was talking about the symbol as though that was the truth of the matter, so that we might someday go flying off into the air without airplanes. No. The air of the spirit. We might say the supersurface level of consciousness, where man belongs. Coming again to that level of consciousness, he is in position to see the surface and the subsurface with perspective. As long as he is on the surface merely, he has his nose in the dust and he doesn't see much – the worm's-eye

view – he understands scarcely anything. He belongs in the supersurface level of consciousness, where there may be the experience of
his true self. It is here that he comes to himself, so that he may
function intelligently on the surface. The spirit of God, the creative
power of life, is then working from above and from below, per-
meating the whole person, and then he is a whole person.

We are very partial people at the moment, aren't we? No wonder
we feel less than we should be, because that's the fact of the matter.
There's nothing wrong with feeling that way. There's nothing wrong
with feeling frustrated or uncomfortable or unhappy – nothing wrong
with that at all. We're bound to feel that way as long as we remain
partial people, as long as we insist upon maintaining this barrier
between the movement of the spirit of God from below and the movement of the spirit of God from above. We're in limbo, caught in
between here, in a world of our own making, an imaginary world, we
might say, which seems so very real to us. But if we begin to allow
these things to work as they are supposed to work, this imaginary
world dissolves and we begin to awaken to the truth.

It is written in the 21st chapter of the Book of Revelation, 'And I
saw a new heaven and a new earth: for the first heaven and the first
earth were passed away,' or dissolved. This layer of distortion in
which human beings now exist needs to be dispelled, and it is not
dispelled by any effort that the human being can make; it is dispelled
when he stops making efforts to dispel it. It's dispelled by the working of the life force, of the spirit of God which is in action now and
has never ceased to act. And we can let it work in ourselves. We let it
work by staying steady at the surface level of consciousness, refusing
to become involved with all the tendencies to react to what is going on
subsurface: the impacts that come upon us out of the environment
and out of our hereditary background. Most people feel these things –
'Oh, but I have to react. I have to do something about this.' We need
to stay steady at the surface level, in the recognition that there is
something working subsurface, and supersurface incidentally, which
we can trust.

Now, in the process by which these changes come there is a need
for those who have some experience in this regard to provide stable
points at the surface. Therefore, if a person begins to sink amongst

the waves of the sea, he can look up and see someone standing there whose hand he can take, just to hold steady while what needs to work out is working out. It isn't done in a moment. After all, how many thousands of years do we have of heredity behind us? And how many years do we have of environmental experiences behind us? All this has to be cleared and sorted out so that what is present in our subsurface levels of consciousness becomes true to the truth; and when that is so, this will rise up to the surface level of consciousness and we begin to see the truth.

If what I am saying to you now is comprehensible to you, in whatever measure, it is because something has happened in your subsurface levels of consciousness so that there is a sufficient transparency, shall we say, clarity, at the surface, to experience what is rising up and what is coming down to meet at that level. 'Let there be light.' This is the way the light appears. We might use the old carbon lamp principle, where there is a positive carbon here and a negative carbon there and they come together like this, with the right gap in between there at the surface. The arc goes across and there's light, brilliant light. Well, this is very scientific, we might say, very exact; nothing of it is by chance. It all works just as accurately at these levels as at those levels where human beings have experience in the external sense. We may cooperate in letting it work or we may resist it. We may try to maintain our own good ideas as to what should be and what shouldn't be, what is good and what is bad. This is what happened, isn't it, according to the story long ago of Adam and Eve. The surface consciousness decides that it is capable of directing affairs here on earth in a manner that will be entirely pleasing and satisfactory; but look at the mess, because it is not capable of itself. There is something working, not only through human beings, not only through animals and plants, but through the whole universe – the same quality of being, the same quality of life, the same quality of spirit, working through everything. Let's let it work through us, then, instead of blocking it. And, of course, if you block life you're dead. We block it a little to start with, and die a little, but we keep it up until that's it!

Why not let what should be a window of heaven be opened at the surface level of consciousness to let something shine down through the supersurface levels of consciousness, and something come up from the subsurface levels of consciousness? Then you begin to have a man – male and female, created on earth – restored to a true state. Now, to understand what that state would be is impossible by the investigation of the surface levels of consciousness. The only way to know what it is is to experience it. We may imagine all sorts of things. We may have some delightful ideas. Some people are inclined to say, 'Well, I like to believe this,' whatever it may be. Well, who cares who likes to believe what? What's the difference? What's the truth of the matter? That's what needs to be known. And we can only know the truth of it because we experience it. We can argue about it until we're blue in the face but it makes no difference. So we're not properly here to argue about anything; we're here to do what is necessary in order to know the truth, to experience the truth, and this comes in a very exact way.

In order to permit this to occur there need to be those who are capable of holding steady, in exemplification of what it is that is required of each one, to let the surface level of consciousness be undisturbed so that it is not constantly enhancing the distortions of the subsurface levels. Let it hold steady for a while and not think it's so important to get all riled up about everything. Such persons maintain a place of calm, so to speak, so that the mind at the surface level of consciousness is held steady, not going off in all directions, not trying to figure everything out, being content, and the heart open toward the real qualities of life itself, which is moving in the individual already, so that there may be a concern to be aligned with these qualities of life, that they may find increased expression. Here they are, ready to come out in every human being but blocked by most people – all people to some extent – by what is immediately subsurface, because there is a habit of behaving in such and such a way. 'I always behave this way. If someone does something in this fashion to me, then I always behave in this fashion in consequence.' And people are puppets in this sense.

Then, here we may become aware of the real qualities of life and be concerned to allow these to find expression. And what we express we know, by the way; that's what we know. Allow the true qualities of life to find expression regardless of what so-and-so does or what someone else says, or what the circumstance happens to be; be the truth of ourselves, in other words. Here is the force that changes things in the world, because it begins to open a window of heaven from the supersurface levels of consciousness through to the subsurface levels of consciousness in human beings everywhere. The working of this power changes what is subsurface, and those changes occur when a person is responsive and open to allow it to happen because he has some integrity. And these things go on without the individual having any real awareness of it. This is the splendid thing about it, because he doesn't have any awareness of it until it reaches the surface. Of course, when it reaches the surface the individual may be inclined to say, 'Oh, now I see, now I know how to do what I should do, and it should be this way and it should be that way,' and immediately he plunges right back down into the mess again. If this force was capable of clearing things so that something does come to the surface, why not let it go on through? Why not let it complete the job instead of again stopping it at the surface? The bright mind says, 'Well, I know how it should be. I know what would make heaven on earth for me.' Do you? Have you been too successful in producing it? Human beings do not know. But there is a knowing. There is a knowing, in the spirit of God, and when we begin to allow our equipment to be operated by the spirit of God, then we share that knowing. We do understand but we don't inject any foolish human ideas into the picture. We let it be the way it is.

Now, obviously, there is a great deal of change to work out, not only in the individual but more so in the world, however it will happen. It will happen through those who are willing to let it happen, and it will happen through those who are not, too, but through them the experience will perhaps not be too happy, because on the one hand there is integration, a bringing together in the true design, and on the other hand there is disintegration, a scattering abroad. These things are happening in an exponential way. There is an exponential experience in the disintegrative sense and an exponential experience in the integrative sense coming. It's here, it's happening, and it's happening in spite of people, at least insofar as the integrative aspects are concerned. It's happening because of people in the disintegrative pattern. But where there is the reality of integrity, where there is a yielding of heart to the truth of being, to the real qualities of life, so that the individual loves these and would be associated only with these, and trusts these qualities in expression and doesn't trust anymore his surface consciousness in its endeavors to manipulate events, trusts this power which is working, which knows exactly what it's doing, and with which we may be associated as we allow it to work through us because we stay steady at the surface levels of our consciousness, then our hearts are open to the beauty, the glory, the wonder, of the qualities and the nature of life itself, that this reality may emerge through us in our living regardless of what the circumstance may be. And when this happens, here is the creative power, here is what is bringing all things to issue now in the world – issue in the creative sense. In that creative pattern it also involves some apparent destructiveness, because the material that is to be used in the creative design must be pried loose somehow from the distorted design.

So we are privileged to share in letting this occur, if we are willing, and we may be assured that there are many others who are participating in the process all across the land.

On Eagle's Wings

Last evening we shared in the reading of a short story about a mouse. This was taken from a book entitled *Seven Arrows,* in which are contained some of the insights and understanding that have emerged out of the traditions of the Plains Indians. This story, while it was couched in terms analogous to a children's story, nevertheless offered an understanding of a very central and beautiful truth. The mice, of course, represented human beings in their present state of experience, the self-centered state, their little mousy noses close to the dust and their little mousy whispers contacting only those things which were immediately at hand. And the mice are always very busy, but obviously in such a situation their vision would be quite restricted. However, this one particular mouse sensed that there should be something more than the usual mousy affairs and consequently was interested in seeking out whatever that more might be. How human beings are trapped in their common experience, most unwilling and uninterested in anything much else! So it has been for countless generations.

Somewhere along the way this particular mouse gained something of a new perspective momentarily by jumping up. His name was changed to Jumping Mouse. He discovered the river and saw the mountain. But of course, when it is merely a matter of jumping, the vision is very brief and the mouse falls back into the old state almost immediately. Here perhaps is a portrayal of the distinction that is maintained between vision and behavior. One may see momentarily and one may subsequently remember what one has seen; but if the vision is based in the jump, then what goes up must come down and the individual is right back where he started, with just a memory of vision. This relates to all human endeavors to rise up, all human endeavors to gain a greater view, a greater understanding, without any essential change of the mousy condition. After all, the creature that jumped up was a mouse and the creatures that were on the ground were mice too, all running around very busily; but occasionally one here or there might glimpse a larger perspective, a greater vision, and might feel rather satisfied because of this, but still behaving in the same mousy ways.

It wasn't until there was a recognition of what was really needed that something began to happen, and what began to happen didn't seem so good to start with – he lost an eye. One aspect of vision in the mousy state began to be relinquished, but why? Because there was a recognition of a need for healing and a desire to play a part in bringing that healing about. We may easily look around us at our fellows, indeed at mankind as a whole, and see a vast need for healing. The nature of that healing, of course, is not perhaps immediately recognized, but if there is a sensing that one may play a part oneself in providing what is necessary, then immediately it becomes evident that one must relinquish something of the view which relates to the past. We have seen this particularly in terms of heredity. Almost all human function is based upon the hereditary influences that are present, coming out of the past. These dominate the mousy existence. Until there is a beginning awareness of the necessity of relinquishing this aspect of dominant control in life the individual must remain trapped in the mousy state. Each generation finds the same experiences arising. Each generation is inclined momentarily to imagine that the experiences are new, something that had never been known by anyone else ever before; but of course it is merely repetitive, based in the backward view, based in those things which are coming out of the past. Much of this is looked upon as being somewhat sacred by those concerned. We have touched upon the mousy idea of what love is, for instance, and this is considered to be very important and must be experienced the way mice do.

✗   So, there is a reluctance in most to lose that eye. In fact, nothing will be done about it until there is a recognition of one's own worth, one's own value, in extending something that has been lacking on earth because one has not been extending it. We can see many lacks and voids everywhere in the world. There are those who set themselves up as judges in the matter, accusing and condemning this one or that one, these people or those people, for failing to fill the voids or the needs; but one only comes into position to lose the eye when the responsibility is assumed for oneself. If you observe a void, an emptiness, if you are aware of this in relationship to your own experience, you are responsible for it, nobody else. It is your observation, after all. It is your experience, nobody else's. Mind you, somebody else may also be aware of the void, but that's his void, his responsibility. Human beings are always trying to push it off on somebody else, but whatever your experience is, that is your responsibility.

There was a willingness on the part of this particular mouse to assume responsibility, responsibility for the necessities of healing, the necessities of changes which need to come. Because of this the healing began to come. The buffalo was healed, but the mouse lost one eye. What a terrible thing! 'If thine eye offend thee, pluck it out.' What a terrible thing! But was it, really? – no, something absolutely essential, that one may no longer remain trapped in the influences which spring forth through everybody out of the past. To start with, a person may not recognize whence the present experience came, but this is where it derives from, and that eye must be lost. There is only one way to lose it, and that is to accept responsibility – a beginning responsibility, of course – for healing, for healing others, for offering something which one may offer oneself alone; but not because one wishes for some satisfaction for oneself. The idea of satisfying oneself by preying upon others comes out of the hereditary past, and all human beings in this present state in the world are parasites in this regard, trying to satisfy themselves by sucking the lifeblood out of others. It is not a very pretty picture and there are not many who are willing to look at it, but it is the fact of the matter – preying upon each other. However, if there is a beginning sense of honor, the individual realizes that he is on earth not to prey upon others but to convey to others something unique, something which nobody else can convey. Only when one begins to move in this direction does he become aware of his own value. The reason most people prey upon each other is because they lack a sense of value, a sense of personal worth, and they imagine they are going to get it from somebody else. This is a very dishonorable attitude and state.

The mouse was willing to lose this eye related to the past. Most are

not. These things have come up in the lives of all human beings in
every generation. There is nothing new about them in any generation,
and every generation has consistently fallen into the same trap. If
there is a mouse here or there who is willing to jump up a little he
may begin to see these things, but for the present just see them; that's
all you can do by jumping up. Various methods of jumping, of course,
have been developed on earth. They come to focus particularly in the
religions of the world. I suppose what is called Christianity is of
greatest immediate concern to most of you, but it includes everything
else. The mice have jumped up in the past and seen something and
incorporated what they saw into their traditions, but they remained
mice. The only purpose of seeing something is to move out of the
mousy condition. There is no sense to seeing anything if you are going
to remain a mouse. What's the point, even though you may be called a
jumping mouse? This is a title of great respect, because there are
many who have jumped up and seen something and then, falling back
down again, have presumed to try to teach other mice what they saw,
obviating the necessity of those other mice jumping up, presumably.
But what foolishness! So the mice remain with their noses in the dirt
and their whiskers twitching with respect to the things around them,
scurrying here and scurrying there, doing this and doing that – how
exciting! – but absolutely nothing being accomplished except the
maintaining of disastrous conditions insofar as mice are concerned.

So, the eye related to the past must go; and then another eye, related to the future presumably, must go too, so that the mouse becomes blind both to past and to future. What would this make
possible? Living in the present, presumably. How much imagination there is with respect to the future! It's all going to come in the
future, isn't it? The good times are ahead! It doesn't really look so
encouraging at the moment. But the mice will triumph, at least hopefully. Evil imagination! Every imagination of the thoughts of men's
hearts is only evil continually. This is an exact description of the
mousy state of consciousness – evil imagination with respect to what
will be, based in what has been. But, relinquishing these two eyes,
the individual becomes freed from these dominant controls of mousy
existence, freed to move toward the experience of a new state.

During the course which this mouse took in his experience, from time to time he became aware of the eagles flying above. Of course, eagles to a mouse look pretty dangerous. One should hide from the eagles lest one be caught. This is the mousy view, isn't it, scurrying around about mousy affairs. What a terrible thing to be separated from those mousy affairs! So the eagles are predators in the mousy view. But the mouse who became blind to past and future, living in the present, was fair prey for the eagle. But do you know what the eagle is? That is the symbol of man, the truth of man. The mouse represents human beings in the state of their present existence, which is a far cry from the truth. Is it such a terrible thing to be caught by the truth? The implication here is that the mouse had no more defenses against the eagle, against the truth of himself. Only the past and the future have been his defenses. He has used them as defenses against the truth of his own being in the present moment, against the eagle. The further implication is that insofar as this particular mouse was concerned the eagle swallowed the mouse. But the mouse became the eagle. That's the case, isn't it? If you swallow a carrot, the carrot becomes you. Is the carrot blessed by becoming you? Not very much if you are a mouse; maybe it was better off as a carrot. But for a mouse to become a man, that is definitely a greater experience. The eagle flies above the surface of the earth. It isn't a matter of jumping up; it's a matter of being there. It is a matter of having keen vision, a perspective outlook, which sees mousy affairs for what they are: of very little meaning or consequence.

A children's story – but like many children's stories it conveys essential truth. We have opportunity of looking at this story from the standpoint of our perspective, and we may see the truth of it. We may see this truth as it relates to our own experience, so that there is a willingness to relinquish the traditions of the past. Traditions are very sacred to many people and there is, generally, an unwillingness to relinquish them. This is perhaps understandable but it maintains the prison. Relinquishing traditions does not mean relinquishing the truth, merely what some human beings thought about it. What they thought about it might have been of value back when they thought about it, if it caused them to begin to move in the right direction, to be willing to relinquish their eyes. We see this very plainly from the standpoint of what has been called Christianity, and also from the standpoint of what has been called Judaism; the Moslems, the Hindus, the Buddhists — they are all in the same boat, all with their traditions, all with their heredities. The usual endeavor is to try to discover what the truth may be and get it to fit into their particular tradition. It won't! The tradition opened the door to the truth, but as long as the tradition is held, the truth is ignored.

There was a man called Paul who lived quite some time ago, quite an intelligent man, well versed in Judaism, and he proposed to fit his understanding of the truth which was brought on earth through the man called Jesus into the pattern of Judaism, so as to correlate them. He has been responsible, to a very high degree, for what has subsequently been called Christianity, particularly the Protestant aspect of Christianity — a tradition, built into the very flesh and marrow of human beings, in certain parts of the world at least, just as the tradition of Judaism has been built into the flesh and marrow of those who call themselves Jews. The same thing is true of those who are involved in the other traditions. But traditions go beyond religion. They relate to all the systematic patterns developed by human beings on earth, and all these things are part and parcel of a person in the physical sense. If this dominates in life one will be just a reproduction of the mice that went before — a terrible sameness about all this, certainly nothing unique, a flat state of nothingness boiling toward complete annihilation. Here is the picture of the mousy world.

This is not the world of the eagle, the eagle who is man, the eagle whose realm is the air, representing spirit, the truth of being. The mice may become one with the eagle, but they won't be flying mice — those are bats. The bats inhabit the belfry. No, the eagle dominates; and that is a different state, a different condition, a different person; it is not merely human. From the standpoint of the truth there is no such thing as a human lord. Someone used these words in a written response as though this was something that had been indicated or taught in this ministry. Maybe from the standpoint of the mousy condition there are those who have titles, such as my own, but that's something to do with mice, not men! From the standpoint of the truth there is no such thing as a human lord. The lord is the eagle. The eagle manifests through human form, yes; here is man. Here is a person who has meaning and value. He is no longer subject to the traditions of men, the built-in traditions. The very compulsions that are present in human beings are included in these traditions, and this is what maintains the mousy state, as long as human beings insist upon being subject to them. Only when a person loses both eyes for himself, the dominant controls out of the past and with respect to the future, so that he comes into the present, can he be taken by the eagle; that is, by the truth. Then he has a new perspective. He has understanding then that was absolutely impossible in the mousy condition. Oh, human beings claim very much for themselves in that condition. They imagine they know so much when they know nothing. Mice know nothing beyond the end of their whiskers; whereas the eagles fly above the earth and know the truth. These two states are impossible to compare, the nothingness of mice and the everythingness of eagles. There is no basis for comparison. Mice are always comparing each other, as though something would be gained by this. One needs to lose the consciousness of being a mouse in favor of the consciousness of being an eagle, and as long as there is a state of being trapped in the mousy condition, the eagle experience is impossible.

Those who rise up on eagle's wings call to the mice, 'Come up hither!' But if the mice are so busy about their affairs, they do not hear. They do not hear the sound, they do not hear the voice, trapped with their own emotions, trapped with their own busy thinking, trapped with their own busy doing. But the voice is heard by those whose busyness no longer so completely dominates. Then there is a recognition of needs here and there and everywhere to be filled by oneself, the healing to be offered in one's own field of responsibility. There isn't a person on the face of the earth who does not have a field of responsibility in this regard – this is particularly true of all those gathered here this morning – a field of responsibility, to give into it what is right and fitting to bless and to heal, not to go along with the traditions. The traditions, in the religious sense, are all earthbound. Judaism is earthbound; Christianity is earthbound. Even those who have been involved with the Emissary ministry have tried, sometimes desperately, to stay earthbound. Holding sacred the things which keep a person earthbound is no blessing; it is a curse. What I have offered over the years has been the open door to freedom from the state of being earthbound. Those who are earthbound end up in the earth underneath the surface, but the eagle is present with respect to each and every one.

Be willing to lose your eyes as mice, that you may be caught by the eagle. And there is nothing disastrous to being caught by the eagle, because you immediately become one with the eagle; you share the eagle's view and the eagle's ability to bless and to heal. Here is the way, the truth and the life so beautifully exemplified by the One who was called Jesus on earth. Let us exemplify this truth in our own living now, in this present moment, not looking to the future, ungoverned by the past, and revealing the beauty of the truth of being now.

The Present Moment

The present moment is hard to find. Presumably, about three or four minutes ago, we initiated this particular service; presumably also, three or four minutes hence this service will still be unfolding. But we find ourselves in between. We could bring it a little bit closer and say that one second ago was the past and one second to come is the future; somewhere in between those two seconds is the present. But we could reduce it still further: a billionth of a second ago was the past and a billionth of a second to come is the future, so the present moment must be less than a billionth of a second. We eventually discover that it is no time at all. In the present moment we move beyond time.

We are all together in the present moment. To the extent that we are consciously present in the present moment, or to whatever degree that this is so, we have moved beyond what might be thought of as the normal world of time and space, because regardless of the geographical distances involved we are all together present in this present moment. Everything narrows down to a point, and here we find again this point which is without magnitude even though we are aware that it has position. It is a point which at the same time is nowhere as well as being now here. In the world of space and time with which we are familiar, it is nowhere, but insofar as our present experience is concerned it is now here.

Perhaps this is what it means when we say it is important to come to point – to find ourselves in the present moment and to discover that in being ourselves in the present moment we are beyond the world of space and time. The present moment has no dimensions and time is not a factor. Time relates to what we call past and future, but we may well say that nothing ever happened in the past and nothing

will ever happen in the future. All happening is in the present. Where
did time go, then?

Of course, we are very aware of what we call time and we are quite
aware of what we call dimensions. We conceive of ourselves as living
in a world of space and time. But this is a conception, is it not?
because when we come right down to it in the present moment we
discover that we are not in the world of space and time. Now, this
may seem a difficult thing to comprehend because we are so accustomed to identifying ourselves as being present in the world of space
and time, as being a part of that, and that this world of space and time
determines what we are. But the facts do not bear this out. The fact is
that we are at this moment, and this moment has no duration. It's still
this moment, isn't it? – exactly between the past and the future, as we
call them, but nowhere and yet now here.

What I am seeking to impress is that in the experience of the truth
of ourselves, of true identity, we are beyond the world of space and
time. It requires a shift in the nature of our awareness to realize this.
We are so thoroughly immersed in what we think of as our experience
in the world of space and time that it seems to be difficult to come to
point in the present moment because our whole experience seems to
be concerned with past and future. And yet insofar as true identity is
concerned, past and future do not exist; everything is in the present
moment. Now, because we have involved ourselves so thoroughly in
past and future, in what we think of as the objective world around us,
we experience a false state of affairs. We have called it the unreal.
That's exactly what it is, because the only reality is this present
moment. As we are restored to the experience of being in this present
moment, we may begin to have a true consciousness of what is
present.

There is something, obviously, which emerges rightly through our
capacities into the world of space and time, but what is happening? Are we not properly, in true identity, in the position of the
creator, generating in consciousness the world of space and time?
Whatever essences may be present in true identity are differentiated
and expanded through our capacity of consciousness and there is
produced a world of space and time. But where? Insofar as the individual is concerned, insofar as you are concerned, it is customary to

think of it as being out there, as being an objective world of reality. But is it? All we know of it is in our own consciousness insofar as we personally are concerned; that is the only place it exists insofar as we are concerned. We interpret it as being an objective world out there, but the fact of the matter is that it is a creation in our own consciousness. That creation, rightly, when we have the experience of being present in the present moment, when we have our true identity in other words, is of the essence of that true identity; in other words, it is a reflection of that, a differentiated expansion of that in consciousness. If we see this, how easily the world of space and time can be changed.

Because in human experience we have left the point of true identity in the present moment and have become involved with what we have thought of as being the objective world around us, our experience of identity has been there and the nature of what is present in our consciousness has consequently derived from this apparent objective world around us, which we have now begun to see is simply a construct in our own consciousness. Something has been constructed in our consciousness and this has been allowed to tell us what we are. It isn't what we are at all, because what we are in true identity is beyond the world of this construct. It is in the present moment where our true identity is. When we are in the present moment, experiencing the reality of that identity, then all that is constructed, created, through us reveals the essences of that true nature. This re-created experience is described as the new heaven and the new earth.

Now, obviously our proper concern is to come again into the present moment in the experience of the reality that is there. This would be describable as oneness with God, wouldn't it? because all true identity is in God and God is in the present moment. God is not in the past. There are many people who think that they are going to find God by looking back into what they call the past, looking back into what is in fact some sort of imagination, because the only reality is in the present. There are others who imagine also that they will find God in the future, that when such and such a thing has worked out, as it might be put, then they will have the experience of what God is. The working out in the future often relates to what human beings call death – after that, then God will be known, or possibly the devil! But there is no past and there is no future, only the present moment, and it takes no time at all to experience what is present in the present moment because the present moment is timeless. ✄

As long as we insist that it is going to take time to experience the truth of being, we insist that we will never experience the truth of being, because the truth of being is beyond time; it is timeless, as the present moment is timeless. You cannot tell me how long the present moment lasts. It is so thin, isn't it? between past and future. It is nowhere in this sense. But we are aware that it really is now here insofar as we are concerned, so what is necessary is that we should leave the world of fantasy and return to the place of reality. In the place of reality there may occur what we might describe as a creative process, a differentiated expansion of what is present nowhere but now here, a new world – a new world which derives from the point of true identity, from God, and is the experience in our facility of consciousness of what that is. Man was created to provide the means by which there might be this differentiated expansion. It's something that occurs in consciousness. Whether it actually occurs in some objective reality around us, we don't particularly need to discuss. We have the experience anyway and it seems that way, but the point is as to the nature of that differentiated expansion.

I am sure that you have had the experience of looking at some object and seeing it thus and so, and then there comes a shift in consciousness and you see the object differently. I recall that a drawing may be made which looks like a chalice. You see that drawing and you say, 'Oh, yes, there's a chalice.' But there may be a shift in consciousness and it no longer looks like a chalice but is seen as two faces looking at each other. How long did that shift in consciousness take? It was instantaneous. It is either one thing or it's the other; you don't see both at the same time. You may flip back and forth, but the flip takes no time at all.

Now it seems that human beings have difficulty in permitting a complete change to occur instantaneously. In other words, there is a flipping in consciousness not too far at a time, a changed outlook which is close to the previous outlook, and then another change and another change. But each change in consciousness occurred instantaneously; it didn't take any time at all. You can't measure the length of it; it's either there or it isn't. Because we are so conditioned to think of things in terms of time and dimension, we see everything happening as a gradual unfoldment, but it isn't. The changes occur instantly or they don't occur.

We have described the changes that take place as the climbing of a mountain, awakening to new positions of observation. We may see this in terms of returning to the point of true identity. In that apparent movement there are instantaneous changes of consciousness, of the way we see things. Now we see something this way; now we see something that way. As we begin to recognize that these things do occur instantaneously we may perhaps begin to emerge from this involvement with the idea that it is going to take some lengthy period of time for anything to happen in our experience. It never does. Our identity, therefore, may begin to emerge out of this insistence that it somehow belongs in the realm of space and time. We have all assumed that it belonged in the realm of space and time. We consider that we have just so many years to live on earth – 'we', our identity! But that isn't our identity at all. The true identity is not hooked to the world of space and time; the world of space and time is, in fact, a creation of true identity.

It has been often said that we are not rightly subject to externals, in other words to the world of space and time. If we are subject, or insist upon being subject, to the world of space and time, we must have a false identity. To experience true identity there is the necessity to let ourselves emerge out of the world of space and time in the sense of identity. I think it was Paul who said that we are in the world but not of it. Perhaps you can begin to see what this really means. We are in the world in the sense of the expanded differentiation of our consciousness, but that expanded differentiation is not what we are. We are at the point which has position but no magnitude whatsoever, no dimensions whatsoever, neither of time nor space.

Our changing state of consciousness, which I suppose might be correlated somewhat with a moving picture film, brings certain new experiences. I use the analogy of the moving picture film because you know very well that this isn't a continuous picture, is it? It's individual frames and there is one individual frame present in the moment. Because of the nature of our makeup, if you multiply the movement of those frames to about twenty-four frames to the second, you don't notice anymore that they are individual frames; it looks as though it's continuous. You know that that is not the case in fact insofar as the moving picture film is concerned. You can think about it; you can sit in the theater and realize that this is the case; but most people don't realize that when they come out of the theater what they observe round about them is exactly the same thing. It simply looks the way it does because of the manner in which our capacities operate.

Jesus, when He was speaking to His disciples, toward the end of His ministry on earth, said, 'I came forth from the Father, and am come into the world: again, I leave the world, and go to the Father.' The 'I' here who was speaking related to the differentiated expression of the One, who was referred to as the Father, the specific differentiated expression which emerged by reason of the man called Jesus. That differentiated expression was a true one. It emerged because the man accepted His identity beyond the world of space and time. 'I came forth from the Father' into the world of space and time, into the realm of consciousness, where this creative process occurs. And, obviously, if this is what is happening, if the differentiated expansion of the true point of identity has occurred, then that differentiated expansion may contract back into the point from which it came. There is no break in its coming forth and there is no break in its return.

This, when it can be seen, reveals the nature of what was called the resurrection, what actually happened. 'I came forth from the Father, and am come into the world: again, I leave the world, and go to the Father.' When it is a true expanded differentiation of the essence that is present nowhere, in God, then there is no distinction between that essence and the source of it. There is no problem insofar as the resurrection is concerned. This is a way of describing something in terms of the world of space and time falsely created by the wrong function of human beings in the realm of their consciousness. Now, this may seem all very obscure, but it only seems so because we are so embedded in our involvement, insofar as our selfhood is concerned, with the world of space and time and we see everything in these terms. But moving out of that so as to come again to the experience of true identity – and it requires that experience to understand – there are certain things that apparently happen.

Obviously, this point in the present moment where true identity is, is a point of stillness. 'Be still, and know that I am God.' What we think of as motion, a succession of these frames moving by, is in the world of space and time. Space and time are necessary to motion. When we come back to the point of true identity it is the point of stillness – no motion. The motion occurs by reason of the processes, the creative processes, by which expanded differentiation occurs. Expanded differentiation is motion but it springs from the point of stillness. Now most human beings, all human beings in the world the way it is now, are in varying degrees involved with all this motion. They're so busy. There's so much to be done, so many things to be experienced, and all this, so that identity is involved with the experience of motion and we seem to imagine all too often that if we really did come to rest there would be nothing: our meaning is based in how fast we can go. Of course, this shows itself in various ways, in the Olympic Games for instance. But then there are fast goings in the realm of the mind also and in the realm of feeling – e-motion. The point of true identity is still; motion occurs in the realm of space and time, which appears to be all around us and we think of it as an objective world. But nevertheless we would have to acknowledge that, while we may think of it this way, that thinking is in the realm of consciousness. We have no real assurance that there is an objective world out there; the only assurance we have is that there is something within the range of our consciousness.

Now, returning to that point of stillness, there are various experiences. Perhaps we need to recognize here that Man is under consideration, and Man is composed of many so-called individual human beings, male and female. The true point of identity is for Man collectively. It may be experienced and should be experienced individually, but individually speaking our experience in that regard will be very closely related to the experience of Man as a whole, because Man was created as a whole and all of us are a part of that. The facility of Man, mankind, is what was created to provide the means by which there could be a differentiated expansion of a specific point of being. That differentiated expansion in the consciousness of Man is creation. Man was created in the image and likeness of God to be one with God, to have the identity of God, and from that identity, nowhere but now here, the creation may occur in the realm of consciousness provided by the capacity of Man. Obviously, if the human experience loses that identity, then there must be the experience of chaos, chaos back of which there is some evidence of order because the identity is still present even though obscured and what has occurred in human experience relates, as we have seen before, to rather a thin layer of consciousness.

Now all this apparent chaos in the realm of consciousness must be cleared. It is cleared as there are those who move back to the true point of identity. One of the experiences that occurs in that movement relates to what we have referred to as the sense of family. We have, I am sure, this morning a sense of family as we may be aware of each other in various places upon this continent. The particular places themselves are lost, are forgotten, but we have a consciousness of being together. Here is an evidence of what seems to be movement toward the point of true identity where there is the experience of oneness. We translate what is occurring in familiar terms, terms familiar in the identification with the world of space and time, and we say 'family' because there are families here apparently and there is a sense of family. But not a family in the usual way exactly, is it? It isn't based in earthly relationships; there is something else; there is something else sensed. And we didn't choose each other particularly; we didn't look each other over and say, 'Well, I like you; I'm going to associate with you.' It may perhaps on occasion have been quite the reverse. We've had some difficulties in our program along that line because people were insisting upon their personal likes and dislikes. 'I don't want to be associated with you.' But we see that what we are talking about now has nothing to do with human wants. We are considering reality. In reality true identity is one. 'The Lord our God is one.' So we come back into that experience if we are to know reality. By reason of that experience of reality there may be the true creative differentiation of the essences of being and there is a new world in consequence, a new world created in consciousness. We may say that what's created in consciousness then takes form, physical form; but what, after all, is physical form? When you begin to analyze it or break it down it becomes atoms and little pieces of atoms, whatever they are – very, very rarefied – and it all begins to vanish into nowhere. It is all, in fact, constructed in consciousness.

Now, because we have fallen so low, we have a very embedded state of outlook and what is seen is not the way it is at all, but we're convinced it is. Of course, one of the things that is necessary is to begin to become unconvinced, to let go, to begin to realize that what we think we have known and seen and believed is in fact nonsense, even though it seems so real. And we may begin to come out of that in what appears to be a movement toward this one place of true identity in the present moment which doesn't seem to exist and yet it does. We need to begin to live from that point rather than in the realm of the expanded differentiation in consciousness. Then whatever occurs in the expanded differentiation in consciousness will be true to the essences in that one point which has position but no magnitude. And 'Behold, I make all things new.'

If we glimpse this, then how easy it really is! But how impossible it is to make things new by struggling with the concepts in the realm of consciousness, both the concept with respect to ourselves and the concept with respect to other people. Gradually we reach a point where we are willing no longer to be moved by these things; in other words, we're beginning to come to the point of motionlessness, stillness, which is the point where we belong. As I say, various experiences come as these specific changes in consciousness occur, and we say we see things differently; the world looks different. But we are, after all, a part of man, so it is not just a matter for the individual – though what is occurring in the individual is a matter for man, because it is changing the state of man. If it doesn't occur in the individual it doesn't occur anywhere; but there is a whole new consciousness to be experienced by man collectively.

This happens by reason of what occurs in individuals in the present moment, by reason of what occurs in you as you let yourselves come again to that point of true identity in the present moment. That point of true identity is not dependent upon anything that you may imagine happened in the past or anything that you may imagine is going to happen in the future. It was not made by motion in consciousness. It was not made, in fact. All that has been made has been made in consciousness, but that from which it was made is not within the range of the world of space and time. Your identity is absolute, not relative. It's not relative to anything. It is an absolute identity here and now, and in that identity what should appear in consciousness appears in consciousness. That we have described as creation.

Be still. We stop being moved by what we have thought of as objective externals, the very things that move everybody, and we reach a point where we can't be moved. Some imagine that that would be inhuman: 'Oh, if you ever experienced that point it would be cold, frigid; it would be. . .' Such concepts derive from ideas present in those who have never had the experience. It seems that way from the standpoint of a false identity in the world of space and time, but it isn't that way. Love is the reality, but no one in that state is moved by what is occurring in his own consciousness; and that's all that he knows of what he thinks of as objective reality: what is occuring in his own consciousness. When you stop being moved by that, stop being governed by that, you may reach a point of stillness. 'Be still, and know that I am' – my true identity – 'God'; my true identity is in God, not in the world of space and time; not in the world of construction in consciousness, but in the here and now, the present moment.

So we come again, by reason of shifts in consciousness, to a new state of experienced identity, the peak of the mountain, which apparently is nowhere but, we realize with increasing clarity and vividness, is now here.

The Eternal Moment

Nothing ever does happen in the future and nothing ever has happened in the past; the only happening is in the present moment. And yet people everywhere are so wrapped up in the past and future that the present moment tends to be overlooked. Yet this present moment is the only moment of reality; everything else is imagination. Now is the only time we can live. We can't live in the past, although some attempt it, and we can't live in the future. We live now or not at all. To the extent that we are drawn out of the present moment we begin to die, because there is no experience of life anywhere else but now. And yet what an elusive point the present moment is, sandwiched, seemingly, between the endless past and the beginningless future so that it appears to be nowhere. However, we know for a fact that it is now here – the moment of living.

There are many people who are very much concerned for the future. Looking at events – which, incidentally, is always looking into the past – these events seem to portend disastrous things in the future, although, with some, hope springs eternal. The hope is that the world will somehow become a better place. Hopes in this regard are fading a little these days, but the quality of the world in which we find ourselves is consequent upon the quality of the human beings who live in it. Of course, speaking of this world, it is a human creation on the surface of this planet; but whatever the quality of the world is, it is simply a reflection of the quality of the people who are present. For some rather obscure reason this doesn't seem to have penetrated the thick skulls of most human beings. They are bound and determined to try to make the world be a pleasing place, carry these qualities of pleasingness, without giving any consideration whatsoever to the quality of the people who dwell on earth.

The most futile of undertakings, as we well may see, is this: to try to cause the world to be anything else than a reflection of the people who live in it. We can't fix the world up to be Utopia while less than Utopian people compose it – a very simple truth, seemingly, but virtually unrecognized, apparently, so that almost all human effort is given, individually and collectively, to fixing the world up so that we may live in peace and prosperity, enjoying happiness and fulfilment for ourselves without in the least being concerned with respect to our own characters and the quality of our own living. Here we see a state of pure insanity – or stupidity, if you like. Who isn't engaged, in the world, in this desperate undertaking to make things be the way we want them to be? Of course our wants vary in particulars, so there is inevitable conflict, and the world reflects the quality of the people in it. What comes first, then: endeavors to devise a suitable political or economic or religious system which will make the world a satisfactory place for us, or to consider what would constitute a satisfactory human being?

A satisfactory human being would not be a human being characterized by present qualities. A change is obviously essential in this area if the world is to change. Nothing that anybody can do to manipulate the world will accomplish anything of any significance whatsoever, except as destructiveness may be thought of as being significant. As long as human eyes are fastened in that direction it is a hopeless situation, logically and obviously so to anyone who honestly looks at it. Unless there is a different quality of human beings present on earth there will not be any different quality of world, so let's leave the world alone and concern ourselves with human beings. Human beings – plural? There is only one human being at the center of our world and that is the one who may refer to him- or herself as 'me'.

Insofar as each person is concerned there is only one human being on earth. That is exactly true. You may imagine that there are multitudes of other human beings; possibly there are – we may call that objective reality. But the only way we think we know there are other people on earth is within the scope of our own consciousness. We can't really prove it, at least not intellectually speaking. We can put up some arguments perhaps, but everything of which we are aware is simply in our own consciousness. So each person, if we are going to put it this way, has his or her own world, peopled apparently by other human beings. And we're all inclined to agree on this point – just as human beings are inclined to agree that little pieces of paper are worth something; they call it money. It's worth less and less these days. But then somebody else says a hunk of metal is worth something and, if everyone agrees, I suppose it seems for the moment to be worth something. But all these things are consequent upon the idea in the human mind. We may say that money is an objective reality – a shrinking reality apparently.

So we have our own worlds, and the quality of the individual world is the quality of the individual whose world it is. 'Oh,' you may say, 'but there are other people in the world who make it the way it is too.' Maybe; who knows? But you are aware of your world and maybe the people in it are of your creation. We could, of course, get lost in abstractions here but this is not the immediate purpose, obviously. Our concern is that the quality of the individual or individuals who produce the world in which we live should become what it ought to be for producing a true world. This is the only way that a true state could be produced – the only way! – and unless the individual who centers the world undertakes to let it be so, it will not be so; and because everybody has become hypnotized into the imagination that the world can be changed by manipulating it, without regard to oneself, the means by which the world could actually change has been completely ignored.

Of course, if anyone looks at it they are inclined to take the attitude, 'You can't change human nature'; in other words, you can't change the quality of human beings. If this is actually the case, then we're condemned. What's the use of doing anything? The quality of human beings sets the quality of the world, so if you can't change the quality of human beings, well, the world's the way it is; why be bothered? Yet there seems to be some sort of aspiration in human beings to try to change the world around; in other words, some awareness that the world is not quite the way it should be. But to acknowledge that the world is not the way it should be because human beings are not the way they should be – this is something that is not readily admitted, at least not specifically with respect to oneself; in a general sense, perhaps, yes, we know we're not perfect, but in a specific sense,

'No!' We dig in our heels; we're defensive immediately: 'Don't you try to change me!' Well, it's not a matter of trying to change somebody else, ever. It is a matter of allowing a new quality of experience in oneself, and a person can only let that happen for himself, if he is the only person present. Everybody else is just peopling his consciousness, so leave them alone.

But here is one person who can let something happen, that person whom individually we refer to as 'me'. 'But you can't change human nature!' All right, why bother with human nature then? Maybe we can't change it because it's not a matter of trying to change human nature, any more than it is a matter of trying to change the world, because the world and human nature are of the same substance. Human nature is a part of the world, obviously, and we're not trying to change the world by manipulation. We are quite content to let the world change because we change, and we do not take the attitude that the world will not change merely because we as individuals change. There are so many people who use the excuse, 'Well, I'm only one person.' That's true enough – just the one person in your world, the one person you know is there. If that one person changes, why wouldn't your world change? You know at least in some measure, from your own experience, that the world does change for you in this fashion. It depends upon you as an individual, and nobody else. So that excuse, 'I'm only one in three or four billion human beings on earth; what can one person do?' is just seen as a . . . what? – duck-out, because you are the only person you know is in your world. Let your quality change, and see what happens.

'Stand still, and see the salvation of the Lord.' This is the way it was put somewhere in the Old Testament. Standing still refers to the nature of the change which must occur: the relinquishing of so-called human nature, that there may be movement out of that, like a snake shedding its skin. When human nature is separated from you it is seen as being as useless as the shed snakeskin; as valueless, as meaningless. So there is no attempt to change human nature or struggle with human nature or to try to make oneself better. Better than what? Better than some other human nature? Is a good human nature better than a bad human nature? They are all human nature, and human nature is what characterizes human beings and therefore determines the quality of the world in which they live; so there is no good human nature, really, or, to put it another way, no right human nature in the sense that the unchanging human nature is thought of in the world. Let it all go, that there may be the experience of something new, something which is real rather than imaginary, because if we live identified with the past and the future, we're living in an imaginary world.

And how human beings like to study the past in various ways – sometimes because if we draw a graph of whatever particular field we may be considering we will see how it worked in the past, how the graph went, and this will tell us how it's going to go in the future, therefore we will be able to be guided by the past with respect to the future. What happened to the present moment? It was lost in the shuffle. The only moment of reality was simply ignored, and human beings trust what they can figure out with respect to the past as being an adequate guide for what should be done in the future. But past and future are totally imaginary. Neither of them ever existed or will exist. The present moment is the only moment there is, ever has been, or ever will be. It is always the present moment – and here is the key, because our guidance does not come out of the past; it comes from the present moment.

Human beings collect information and knowledge, which all comes out of the past, doesn't it? There's so much of it in the world now that no human mind can encompass it all. And every year it's being multiplied, isn't it? – more knowledge, more information piled up. The libraries are full of it. It's in the computers, in their memories – all this mass of stuff coming out of the past, as though that were the basis for living. It isn't. Life is of the present moment, not of the past. Life can only be experienced now. Knowledge is not life. Knowledge may be looked upon as a part of human nature, I suppose, that we're going to let go of. Human beings get all this knowledge and then they devise theories about it, philosophies of all sorts, as to how we should live to make the future better – the future which doesn't exist, never will exist, patterned on a past that never existed! That all relates to human nature, which, from this standpoint, I suppose, we could say never existed either. It shouldn't be hard to let go of, then.

But there is the present moment in which we may have a present experience, and here we have recognized something with respect to the reason for human existence. Human beings make possible the translation of whatever is in the present moment into the form and expression of this dimensional world in which we live. The present moment, from the standpoint of this dimensional world, seems to be nowhere. The past and the future, after all, occupy all the space. Where's the present moment? But we know it is now here – to translate what seems to be nowhere into the dimensional form of the now here.

Now, I say, it 'seems' to be nowhere because a point, as we have noted, has position but no magnitude, no magnitude whatsoever; therefore it's beyond the world of dimensions. The present moment is beyond the world of dimensions and we belong in the present moment. We belong beyond the world of dimensions, or, we might say, at the apex point of the dimensional world, the point that has position but no magnitude. It has position because it's everywhere, or, on the other hand, we could say it's nowhere. There is nowhere where the present moment is not the present moment; I don't care where you go. We talk about the far reaches of the universe whence light comes to us at immense speed. Even so, it takes millions of years to get to us. Does that mean that that must be the past out there? Of course not. It's the present moment out there, just the same as it is here. What has the speed of light got to do with it? The present moment in this sense is everywhere, and yet when we try to define it, it seems to be nowhere. Ah, it's now here, and we're now here.

We're in the present moment. We can relinquish the past. We need not be concerned about the future; it's never going to come anyway. But we have the experience of the present moment, and that's all that counts, because we have the capacity to translate the essences that are present in this point of nowhere, or now here, into the forms of this dimensional world which, incidentally, occupies our consciousness. The point of identity where we belong is now here, nowhere else, and there is something now here to spring forth into dimensional expression because we individually are now here. In other words, what takes form in this dimensional world rightly comes through the present moment. It doesn't come out of the past; it doesn't come out of the future; it springs forth from this present moment. Therefore, within this present moment where our point of identity belongs are the essences of all the qualities which need to take form because we are now here. It's all present, waiting to be born.

Life is born in the moment through the individual. That's true; we know it; we have the experience of it. It has ever been so. And in that focus point of identity there are the essences of all that can take form because we individually are now here. Just as the oak tree is in the acorn, so is the world, the universe, in this present moment at the point of true identity. Human beings have been talking about this in various ways all down through the ages, but apparently never really seeing it in any meaningful sense. The word *God* is used to describe this unknown point which is beyond space and time. Because we call it a point, does that mean that it is nothing? It's only a point from the standpoint of those who define things in dimensional terms. The only way it can be known as to what it really is is to be there. And human beings have looked at God, and maybe worshiped God, believed in God or disbelieved in God, whatever He is, something somewhere, they didn't know where. Well, of course not, because God cannot be known in the dimensional world until there is someone who translates that point into the now here of the dimensional world. Then He is known; otherwise He is beyond the dimensional world and is unknown.

It requires human beings to know God if God is to be known in the dimensional world. Human beings – who, after all, are dimensional people – cannot squeeze through a point that has no magnitude to get into some other . . . what? Where is it? Nowhere. But from the standpoint of our sense of identity we can be at that point, and then, of course, we are in position to say, and speak truly, 'I am' – simply that, a statement of being: 'I am.' At that point all the essences are concentrated, but dimensionally speaking we don't know what they are until they are translated into the dimensional world. Here are the essences of the true quality of the individual waiting to be differentiated, and it is not for the mind to try to figure it out. How could it? There's nothing to figure out. Whatever it is that is to be figured out is nowhere, so how can we figure it out? All we can figure out is what we imagine happened in the past. We collect all that information, store it away, then bring it forward and say, 'This is going to guide us now as to what we're going to do in the future.' And on the basis of all this information, all these things we've learned – what did anyone ever learn insofar as living is concerned? We learn to die! But on the basis of all these things we've learned, we're going to be so wise, we're going to have such big heads, that we're going to be able to function just perfectly in the future. Of course it will take a while yet; a few more thousand years, maybe millions of years, of evolution are going to get it done. Nonsense! Fairy tales! Figments of fancy that simply exist nowhere but in human imagination. The god of human beings, apparently, has been the knowledge of the past, which is going to give us the required information for the future. So we believe implicitly in this god – 'Tell us more! Tell us more, and then we'll be able to do great things tomorrow.' Childish nonsense, and yet seriously engaged in by millions of people.

The true God is the God of nowhere who is nevertheless now here, now here capable of being experienced in the present moment, capable of being experienced in a personal way. This is what makes God personal. Human beings have thought of Him as being a person, and then they tried to make Him into some sort of vague law or mind or something that permeates everything. But the only way that God is known is as a person, because it requires a person to translate what is beyond the world of space and time into the world of space and time; so it's a very personal translation, and when it's done you know what it is. If you don't do it you don't know what it is, and then you feel that you must, well, somehow believe in a God somewhere – but apparently nowhere!

All that is essential to living is concentrated, we might say, in the present moment. If we move out of the present moment and become involved with the past, to that extent we die. The present moment is eternal. There are some people who are hoping to get into eternity. Usually they hope they'll get into it after they're dead; but life is in the present moment. The present moment is eternity, obviously so. There has never been any other moment. There never will be. Here it is; here we are, concerned, rightly, to be still in this present moment, having relinquished the dimensional human nature in favor of the experience of a true identity in the present moment, the identity which is God, or in God, or however it might be put. We have to speak in parables of some kind because, from the dimensional world standpoint, we are speaking about nowhere and no thing. But the nowhere and the no thing become now here and all things when we are in that point and therefore allowing a correct translation to be made so that what before had no magnitude is now given magnitude. We magnify the Lord, the Lord who is nowhere. We magnify Him in the now here because we begin to come to rest in the present moment. We stop stewing about the past and the future as we learn to abide in the present moment and provide correct translation of what is emerging in the present moment – the oak tree – out of the seed.

It isn't anything that can be figured out by the human mind. The human mind is useful when it is sufficiently relaxed and capable of translating correctly. There is a rhythm to these things. Some of you may have been aware of the recent World Figure Skating Championships. One of the skaters, a Canadian – what's his name? – Toller Cranston, is perhaps the most outstanding skater in the world, but he came third in this competition because he messed up the compulsories, as they are called. In other words, when something was imposed upon him it disrupted his natural rhythm. Various reasons, no doubt, are given as to why this happened, but basically, in this particular field, he was not capable of handling what seemed to be an imposition. It wasn't his rhythm, so he made a mess of it. But when he was allowed to be free in his own rhythm, then there was a perfect translation.

This perhaps pictures something with respect to what I've been talking about. There are rhythms that are natural, and we should learn to move with those rhythms. But at the same time we are in a world that is in a very disrupted state, so we need, while being attuned in the true rhythms, to be able to handle the rhythms which seem to be imposed upon us; not to fight against those rhythms, which is basically what this man did, but to handle them, connect them up with the natural rhythms so that they can be handled rightly.

We must learn to do this in our daily experience, and the assistance that is needed for a person to come to the point where he returns to this present moment in true identity is what may be called, rightly, education. Education is a process of drawing forth, drawing forth what already is present, present in this point. The essences are all

there. The trick is to let them be drawn forth, to let them be translated, and that requires education. It requires some assistance to
begin to be capable of allowing this process to happen, so that the
trust is in this focalized point of essence rather than in all this mass of
information and knowledge with which we are constantly being in-
undated. Human beings trust that. They trust what they think they
know in their minds and try to direct themselves on this basis, and
there's a mess. We have the world of the quality it is because of this.
But when we learn to permit the essences that are present in the
present moment to expand through us into the dimensional world, we
move with the rhythms of being, which are the rhythms that are
moving throughout the whole universe. We are part of the universal
ecology then, and that is life. That's what life is.

Of course, the mind then gets busy and says, 'Well, what about this
and what about that? Answer this question. Answer that question.
How can this be?' We do not have minds in order to ask questions.
That's heresy, isn't it? That's why everybody thinks he has a mind, to
ask questions, to get information, to get more knowledge, which we
don't need. The mind is not for asking questions. The mind is a
means by which answers are given. If the mind is occupied with
asking questions, it can't give any answers. No, the mind is part of the
dimensional means by which what is nondimensional may be translated into the dimensional world, and that translation is the answering of questions, so that everything may be known, seeing that the
present moment is eternal. Using dimensional terms, we'd say, 'Well,
there's lots of time.' We call it time, but actually the point of our true
identity is beyond the world of time and space.

We are in the world of time and space but not of it – beyond it, at
the crossover point between what seems in the world of time and
space to be without dimension . . . between that realm, whatever it is,
and the realm of dimension. We're at the crossover point. That's where
our identity belongs; not all wrapped up in the hereditary past, not all
wrapped up in the hopes for the future, but at point now here.
And in that position the world for which we provide the centering
point individually is transformed, reflecting the quality that is inherent in the reality defined by the word *God*. That's a perfect world,
inhabited by perfect people – but not perfect people according to the

ideas of some human mind. The human mind has no idea what perfect people would be. It only knows what perfect people are when they are. Then there they are – no dispute, no reason to question; there's the answer. Let us share in giving that answer because we come to point in the present moment in a conscious awareness of the life, the quality of life, that is now here.

The Mountain

'I will lift up mine eyes unto the hills, from whence cometh my help.

'My help cometh from the Lord, which made heaven and earth.'

These are the first two verses from the 121st Psalm. The hills, or the mountains, have provided a symbol to human consciousness of whatever it is that is higher than man. This which is higher he has called *God*, in the English language at least. In human consciousness the word *God* refers to something unknown. It may have been intellectually defined by some, or refer to something that is felt by others, but God remains unknown as long as man is looking toward God. In human identity God is seen as being separate from oneself, and so He remains mysterious and unknown; He must be accepted on faith or rejected on faith. In true identity the word *God* would refer to something that is known, known because there is no separation between God and man.

The mountain has been used to portray what is higher than man. The peak of the mountain, particularly, is the place of the unknown God. Why does the mountaineer wish to reach the peak? Rather uncomprehendingly, it has been said that the mountain must be climbed simply because it is there; but the peak of the mountain symbolizes something to the mountaineer. The mountain, of course, is a challenge to him, but why is he challenged that way? Because in human consciousness there is the aspiration to come again to God; the mountain peak symbolizes the place of God. We have considered how Mount Zion has been used in the Bible to portray this same thing, and it has always seemed to people that God somehow dwelt high up. It has been imagined that advanced spiritual beings of some kind lived in the tops of certain mountains: Mount Shasta, for instance, in California; the Himalayas perhaps. But all this was related to the fact of a memory in human beings of something higher, a higher state of being; not for someone else but for oneself.

Using the symbolism of the mountain in this way, it can be seen that most people dwell on the plain. If you lift up your eyes when you stand upon the plain and look toward the mountains, from that position they are very impressive, very majestic. This is the way that human beings have looked toward God. The mountains are far off and human beings have felt that they were condemned to live on the plain; in fact, most probably never even raised their eyes to see the mountain, they were so engrossed in what was occurring at their feet. This is the way that human beings go, isn't it? – down. You go in the direction in which you look. You don't really back up the mountain! No, human beings see the same old round. Having been born into this world, they get an education, they get a job, they get married, they get sick, they die! What futility, and yet generation after generation human beings follow out the same ridiculous round. This fills the human horizon apparently; but you know, I am sure, that there is far more quality and capacity in you than could possibly be expressed in such a prison cell. Your eyes have been raised from that to catch a glimpse of the mountain.

Those dwelling on the plains who do raise their eyes to see the mountain apparently have a rather good view of the mountain. This is what is called faith in God. There are those who, seeing the mountain, have imagined that all that was necessary was to dwell on the plain and look at the mountain. They felt they were better, or superior, probably, to those who merely looked at their feet. But whether one looks at one's feet or at the mountain – these are the two alternatives – both still dwell upon the plain; so what's the difference? Of course, those who look at the mountain may aspire to climb the mountain; if you don't look at the mountain you'll never climb it.

As the mountain is approached its apparent majesty becomes less, and there are those who have become troubled by this appearance of things. If a beginning is made of the ascent of the mountainside, the mountain itself vanishes. Those who are prone to judge by the appearance then may say, 'I'm worse off now than I was before. At least when I was out on the plain I could see the mountain, but now I don't know where it is. Maybe it doesn't exist.' Such an attitude is really rather peculiar, isn't it? because here the person is, standing upon the slopes of the mountain, and yet he is less convinced than he was before that the mountain exists. He was more sure of its existence when he was way off from it somewhere and just saw it sticking up out of the plain. Maybe that was an optical illusion, a mirage. Is it not more surely there in one's own experience when one comes to stand upon the slope of it, even though the peak cannot be seen anymore?

The perspective changes. What becomes more visible is the plain. As you rise higher on the mountainside you may look out across the plains and you see the plain for what it is – flat. You behold the dwellers on the plain in their troubles: troubles which are consequent upon the fact that they dwell on the plain. And yet they mill around on the plain trying to get rid of their troubles, while remaining on the plain – an impossible task. On the plain the human experience is of a human identity. In human identity God seems to be afar off, if He exists at all. For those who recognize the futility of existence on the plain of human identity, and proceed to the foot of the mountain with the intention of climbing it, there comes the feeling of being somehow different from the plain dwellers, and the plain dwellers see the mountaineers as being a bit peculiar. So many people are satisfied, or think they are, in the state of human identity, existing in a little two-by-four cell, going down. To go down on the plain you just have to dig a hole, and most human beings spend their lives digging their holes; and eventually, of course, someone else has to fill the hole in, with the original digger underneath. This is the customary practice on the plain of human identity.

But who doesn't have a sense of a potential of something far greater? If you look in the direction of the plain of human existence, that's where you will exist as long as you last; but if you lift up your eyes unto the hills, then perchance you will move in that direction and begin to leave behind the futility of the human plain of existence. To some, momentarily it may seem to be more or less comfortable on the human plain of existence. The trap of technological advances has raised what has been called the standard of living; and that is a trap, because it causes people to imagine that this is satisfactory. Of course, fortunately, the satisfaction tends to be rather short-lived. This is becoming more apparent in these days. It has apparently been assumed that what human beings have supposed progress to be would go on forever: technological expansion, more stuff made, more stuff consumed, more satisfaction. But it doesn't go on forever; time and material run out. The standard of living is not really a standard of living at all; it is simply a standard of dying. Victory is conceived to be the ability to die in comfort, seeing that we are going to have to die anyway, and so we have developed a high standard of dying. But now this is threatened and we may be required to die in misery. Perhaps what is happening may cause others of the plain dwellers to lift up their eyes unto the hills. We may trust so; but whether they do or not, the mountain remains, and the peak of the mountain is the true dwelling place of man. He is not rightly a dweller on the plain of human existence.

Some of those who have lifted up their eyes unto the hills have been drawn to the hills and started the ascent. And for them, as has been noted, the external view of the mountain has consequently vanished. Yes, some complain a little about this. 'I had more faith when I was on the plain,' they say. They saw the mountain then; it seemed to be safer to dwell away from the mountain and just look at it, enjoy the spectacle, the beauty, the majesty, the glory. But this has maintained the condition of human existence just as surely as was the case for those who merely looked at their feet. All have been in the same boat. The only thing was that those who had raised their eyes might possibly have come to recognize that the mountain was real and not merely a distant mirage which had to be accepted on faith. Then, having the courage of their convictions, they began to move to the mountain and to stand upon the lower slopes, feeling the solidity of the rock under their feet. When this was sensed there was no need anymore to see the mountain as such, because to this extent it was being experienced. It was no longer a distant hope; it was underfoot, something was being known in experience. If one then reverted to the viewpoint of the plain dweller, saying, 'Well, I should be able to see the mountain,' he would again come down to the plain of human identity and be worse off than he was before: he still won't see the mountain and neither will he be standing upon the lower slopes of it.

For those who begin to ascend the mountain, remember that the experience is different to that of those who merely stand upon the plain, and the awareness of God is different. The full reality is not yet known, of course, but something is known because of the place where one stands. If you are actually standing upon the slope of the mountain, you are upon the mountain, if not yet upon the mountain peak, and because of this the mountain is real to you; it does not require any more faith to believe it. Faith is only required by those who dwell upon the plain, but here is a different experience. For the moment it may not seem to be much improvement over what was known upon the plain, but in fact the ascent of the mountain toward the peak has begun.

Continuing to move upward, then the plain begins to be spread out below and there is a new view as to what is occurring on the plain. I am sure that you have experienced this. The very fact that you have a perspective which is different from that of the plain dwellers is evidence of movement up the mountainside. For the moment, this is about all the external evidence you have. You see, the slope goes on ahead but you can't see the mountain and you can't see the peak. But you can see the plains; you can see the plain of human existence and begin to understand what that is. You had prior experience out there on the plains and now, standing upon the slope of the mountain, you can look back and over and see the plains spread out, with all the dwellers thereon, and you understand what is occurring out there and how human beings have been trapped in that condition in human identity, never coming to know their true identity. You see the falseness of it all and perhaps it saddens you, because you are aware of many good, well-meaning people involved in that state, trapped in it. They think they do not know which way to turn; they feel helpless and hopeless. You realize that, and you also realize that many are there who are self-satisfied, have deluded themselves into imagining that they are contented – all this mass of human beings existing in human identity, lost, but, insofar as many of them are concerned, unaware that they are lost. The condition experienced in that state has become so customary that most take it for granted. Taking it for granted, they throttle their own true greatness. They despise themselves because there is an insistence upon remaining in the trap, and in the trap what a person really is can never find release and expression; it only comes because there is movement out of that state up the mountain.

Long ago it was said that Moses ascended the mountain to receive the Law. What he received he brought again to the people but found them completely disinterested in the Law, in the truth. They were interested in their golden calf and the worship thereof. Here again is the portrayal, the symbol, of the mountain, and the Lord God who dwelt upon the summit. This is a true picture, a true portrayal, conveying something to the consciousness of human beings, but what the portrayal is really can only be known by those who actually experience what it is. It is useless to have some intellectual definition or merely some deep feeling conviction. The actual change from being a dweller of the plains to a dweller on the mountain peak must occur if what is thereby portrayed is to be understood. Merely to read or consider fables achieves little. Only those who actually move begin to know the truth.

Moving up the mountainside requires relinquishing the habits of the plains. The arbitrary rules and regulations which are required to maintain some semblance of law and order on the plains must be relinquished in favor of the character of the mountaineer. As I say, the select few out of the body of humanity who, in the physical sense, climb mountains are looked upon as being a little bit odd by the rest of the people. Why undertake something so strenuous and so dangerous and so difficult if you can be comfortable on the plain? So it is for those who move, in the sense of what is thus symbolized: they are seen as peculiar, a peculiar people. But here is the return to the true state of man, who was not created to be a dweller upon the plain of human existence.

Ascending the mountain he loses sight of the mountain because he no longer sees the mountain separate from himself. Only the plain dweller sees the mountain as being somewhere else. Those who are moving up the mountain slope do not see the mountain as being somewhere else. It is where they are. Gradually the consciousness of the mountain increases as height is gained. As height is gained, perspective enlarges; it is possible to see further out over the plains. And because of the increased height the consciousness of the mountain increases. A person may say to himself, in sudden awareness, 'I am upon the mountain.' If you are upon the mountain, the mountain is real to you. If you are merely looking at it from afar off it isn't real: it may be there or it may be just hallucination. But if you are standing upon the mountain, you know it; you know the reality of the mountain, and you begin to experience the fact that you are not separate from the mountain. The only way you could separate yourself from the mountain would be to come down it and go out onto the plain again; but to one who has begun the ascent of the mountain, surely that would be unthinkable.

There is the acceptance of the fact that there is a difference between the one who ascends the mountain and those who dwell on the plain. If there is emotional involvement and intellectual involvement with those who dwell on the plain, you will never ascend the mountain and it will remain just a fancy. There will be the question as to whether there really is a mountain or not. There will be a question as to whether there really is a God or not. Who can tell? Some believe in the mountain, some believe in the soil of the plain, but who knows? Only those who stand, first of all, upon the slopes of the mountain; then they begin to know. Woe unto them should they deny that knowing! If you base your consideration of God upon what you saw when you were standing on the plain, you will be lost. If you try to believe in God in that fashion you will say, 'Well, I don't know. Is there a God or isn't there? I can't see the mountain.' But if you base your consciousness of God in the mountain upon which you stand, at whatever level, then you know the truth of it.

So much questioning arises, in the consciousness of those who are moving up the mountainside, which is based on the vision that was only possible when they were standing on the plain. That vision isn't possible anymore. It is a different experience now, and part of the consciousness of the reality of God is consequent upon the perspective view that is obtainable from the mountainside. When you see what is around you on the plain and begin to comprehend what is happening out there – not just in theory but recognizing what is occurring in specific human lives and in the pattern of the nations – as you begin to see this, that is your consciousness of God. It isn't a fanciful belief in a great majestic mountain off there somewhere anymore; it is an actual experience of seeing what is around you from the level at which you are on the mountain. To that extent you see through the eyes of God. If you see through the eyes of God, God is a reality to you. That is the reality, the vision that you have.

That isn't a complete vision, by any manner of means, yet, because you are still on the slopes of the mountain and the complete vision is not available until you reach the peak. Moving up the mountainside there will be an inadequate awareness of oneness with God because such awareness as you have is bound to be limited both by the level on the mountain where you are and also by reason of the particular side of the mountain where you are. So there is no objection to the fact that there are certain limitations to your state while you are moving up the mountain, but the very fact that you have new vision and changing vision is an indication of your oneness with the mountain. Don't deny it. Don't deny that merely because you don't see what you would see from the peak of the mountain. Let the upward movement continue because you have assurance of what is under your feet. You wouldn't have risen up to see the world in a different way if there wasn't a mountain under your feet. It couldn't otherwise be done. You're not suspended in the atmosphere. We weren't built to float around that way. Our feet stand upon the mountain; because of that, we are not separate from the mountain.

Coming to the peak, we discover that we are what is at the peak. That's logical, isn't it? When we come to the peak, we are at the peak. Human beings have sometimes used the words 'I am' to indicate the true nature of God, and there are those who have referred to *the* 'I am'. If you refer to *the* 'I am', obviously whatever 'I am' is is separate from you. You are pointing to something else; the 'I am' which is at the peak of the mountain. But who is that 'I am' when you are at the peak of the mountain? 'I am that I am!' The ascent of the mountain brings that transitional experience between human identity and true identity, but if our feet are firmly planted upon the mountainside we are then standing upon the mountain and in season we may stand upon the peak. It is at the peak that there is no separation between God and man; the individual may say, 'I am that I am.' From that vantage point, where would you look for God? There would be no more seeking God, as though He were somewhere else.

'That where I am, there ye may be also.' That would be a statement from someone standing on the mountain peak: 'Be here with me and know God.' Then God is no longer the unknown God, for what is meant by that word is known. That is the true state of man. That provides the true identity of man. Obviously, it would be foolish arrogance for someone to stand upon the plain and say, 'I am that I am,' saying in effect, 'I am God.' When people do that, standing on the plain, they are usually removed to an institution – rightly so.

There must be movement up the mountain. We have the opportunity of knowing such movement and of proving such movement in our own experience by reason of the nature of our vision with respect to the world around us. If we only see the world around us as a plains dweller does, we don't see anything, we don't understand anything, we're trapped. We may fool ourselves in that condition but we remain imprisoned and we never know the truth. But the truth immediately becomes known to us the moment our feet stand upon the slopes of the mountain; not the whole truth but the truth that is made apparent by our vision, our vision of the plains from the mountainside. If you have any new vision in that regard, you stand upon the mountainside; never deny it. There is no reason to try to have faith in God; your feet are upon the mountain, upon the rock, and your vision proves it. Be true to what you know, then, and do not try to make your knowing conform with some concept that you may have had and others may have had as plains dwellers. It is a new state, something different; and this is the process, of course, by which the fulfilment of those words, 'Come out of her, my people,' is brought to pass. Those who ascend the mountain come out of the grave, the valley of the shadow of death, where the dwellers of the plains abide.

The Mountainside

The analogy of the mountain is most effective in many ways; as with any analogy, however, it only provides a clear portrayal in a certain area. As long as we are considering that particular area, then the understanding is available, but always there are aspects to any analogy which fall short of providing a true picture in the complete sense. For instance, climbing a mountain may give the impression of a rather arduous task requiring a great deal of struggle and effort. In order to bring understanding of what is actually the case, some other analogy would be needed to encompass this particular aspect because the idea of mountain climbing gives a false picture.

We have considered the changes that rightly come as there is movement away from the plain of human identity, as being in the nature of an awakening, an awakening to something that was already present. In this sense the whole mountain is already present insofar as each person is concerned. It is a part of what he is. If one's experience is limited to human identity, then the reality of that mountain is not known; but there is, properly, what may be described as movement from one state into another, and in that movement there is awakening.

When human beings think about awakening, however, it is usually thought of as a one-shot deal: 'I was asleep; now I am awake.' But in this particular area of consideration it is not so. Likewise, there has been the thought that rebirth was a one-shot deal. The individual in the Christian world may say, 'I am now a born-again Christian' – whatever that would mean. But rebirth is a repeated experience. We have noted in this connection that conception is a birth. What is called birth in the usual sense, of course, is another point of birth, but there are subsequent points of birth thereafter: a baby becomes a child, a child becomes a youth, a youth becomes an adult. The natural

state of affairs involves repeated births. So there are repeated awak-
enings – awakening to a new level on the mountainside; not that one
has struggled up to that level, but merely awakened to the reality of
it, so that at whatever level one may be awake, that is the level from
which observation takes place and it determines what may be seen.

One can see what is at the level where one is, and one can see what
is below that level, but one cannot see what is above. There may be a
hint of what is above, but until one moves in awakening to that new
level, one cannot really see from that level. The awakening relates to
vision from a particular level. If one has not awakened to a higher
level, one cannot see from that level; one can only see from the level
at which one is awake, and one may see what is below that level. If
you are thoroughly embedded in the material realm of physical function, that's just about all you will see.

We have some awareness that we live in a world that is more than
a physical world; in fact, we have noted that there is a seven-
dimensional world. There are seven planes, or seven levels, in this
sense. Again, this is rather an arbitrary statement, because you can't
really put a line of demarcation between any of the levels; they merge
into each other, just as the colors of the rainbow do, and yet we say
there are seven colors. In fact, there are many more than seven, but it
is convenient to classify them in this fashion – and so with these levels
of being which are capable of being experienced by us.

We have experience of the first-plane level, the physical level; and
some people are very much wrapped up in that, and everything they
see is conditioned by this viewpoint. Others rise up a little higher and
occupy themselves with some mental activity. They see things
differently; the physical is conditioned by their mental view of it.
And so it goes as there is movement from level to level; one sees a
greater depth. The higher you rise the deeper you can observe. But
until the mountain peak is reached, the seventh-plane level, observation is bound to be incomplete. Those who function in the first two
planes of being without much regard to anything else are usually very
opinionated. They have set views about everything. Of course most of
the views that human beings hold are developed from other people's
views. Sometimes someone else's view is swallowed whole. As there is
an awakening at higher levels on the mountainside it becomes quite

apparent that one's previous view, before that awakening, was a limited one and, because of that, a distorted one. So perhaps the quality of tolerance puts in an appearance. One becomes increasingly aware that one doesn't know it all and that opinions formed while one is still on the mountainside will always be incomplete and distorted, so why form them in the first place?

There begins to be the awareness of one's own incompleteness of vision; and, of course, with respect to those whom one may observe functioning at a lower level, that incompleteness of vision is most obvious. But usually those who are functioning at those lower levels don't realize that their viewpoint is distorted and limited. People are inclined to affirm their opinions with great force. One may suspect that the force that is used is commensurate with the lack of assurance that the opinion is right; nevertheless human beings are inclined to hold these firm opinions. But what nonsense! It's all foolishness, because what is really there cannot be seen until it is all seen. If one just sees a little piece it will not bring any very adequate understanding. One may develop theories, of course – like finding a little bit of bone, so someone builds a dinosaur. But there is no need to speculate, no need to try to develop theories about things or to build models of what we suppose to be the case. Nothing is gained by it, because it is all make-believe. When we reach the point where we could build a true model, we don't need to, because we see the picture and there is no need for a model. So the adequate vision can only be experienced on the mountain peak. Until that is known, what we see will be an untrue picture to some extent. If the complete picture is the seven-dimensional one, then if we see only from the standpoint of two or three dimensions, obviously it's not going to be true to life. So we develop a tolerant attitude and we are not so sure that we are always right.

One is in position to see what is present at the level where one is and below. On the side of the mountain it is impossible to see the mountain peak. There are those who have endeavored to see me as though I were on the mountain peak. That would be impossible, wouldn't it? because anyone can only see me at the level where he is; therefore, insofar as that person is concerned I am at that level. That's all he can see. As there is an awakening to higher levels on the mountainside, then the view of me changes, but do not try to project me to the mountaintop. Returning to the analogy of the mountain climbers, there may be a guide who perchance may have climbed to the top of the mountain before; but, regardless of that, insofar as the party he is guiding is concerned he will be at the level where they are. Perhaps he may be leading the way, he may be a little higher, but all the members of the party are roped together. One always sees at the level where one is. Sometimes people have imputed something tremendous to me; sometimes people have imputed something not so good to me; but whatever the level of the individual who observes, so will his imputations be. However, this makes no difference to me!

In considering this matter of being able to observe only from the level where one is, it may be recognized that if one is moving up the mountain one will continually be seeing very much the same things but in a different way. So many people are anxious to see new things; but we don't see new things; we see things new – the same things, but they are new because they take on added dimensions. According to our level on the mountainside so will the depth of our vision be, including all the dimensions that are below us but excluding all the dimensions that are above. I have sometimes thought that if there is really progress being made in this sense and we are awakening to new levels together, I need only give one service; everybody can read it again in two weeks' time, and then after that in two weeks' time! As there is movement up the mountainside the understanding with respect to the service will change; it will be discovered that there are more dimensions than had at first been thought. One of the problems, if you can call it that, with respect to giving services is that those who hear are hoping for something new. No, the same something but seen from a new level. Maybe our vision needs to encompass more – and it will, as the perspective from the mountainside changes – but basically we see the same things from a new standpoint. Our vision will include what we saw from the old standpoint, but another dimension will be added.

So there is no longer this frantic search, which occupies so many people, trying to find something new. There is no need for anything new in that sense; just for a person standing in a different position to look at it. As there is an awakening to a higher level on the mountainside, then a new person is standing there, not the one who was before asleep to that level. That person is now awake, so there is a new person there; and because there is a new person, what he observes is new even though he is observing the same thing as before. Most people expect that if they are to make spiritual progress they are going to somehow penetrate into a realm of deep, dark mystery; they are going to get away from things, the things to which they are accustomed, through a little hole somewhere, I suppose, into a realm that is totally new. This is the idea of going to heaven, isn't it? When a person dies he is supposed to somehow get away from things into this totally different realm. But the truth is that our experience is where we are, not where we aren't; and according to the level at which we are awake, so is the nature of our awareness, and this is how we see what is to be seen. What is to be seen is far more than we have seen but it is not separate from what we have seen. It is not as though one could say, 'Well, let's forget everything we have seen and turn around and we will see something that we have never seen before.' We do see things that we have never seen before but only in relationship to what we have seen before. We are not traveling to some mysterious, mystical realm elsewhere. Where is 'elsewhere'? The only 'where' we know is where we are, and what we know where we are is dependent upon the extent of our awakening, the place where we stand on the mountainside.

Not only do we become tolerant from the standpoint of our own views, recognizing that they are incomplete, not trying to foist them on somebody else, but we become tolerant about other people's views, because we know they can only see from the level where they stand. We can't make them see from any other level. Let them see from that level; that's fine, we don't object. However, if we are functioning from a higher level, or are capable of doing so, we can provide the guidance necessary to those who are willing to move to a higher level. But we always start from the level where the person is; we don't try to make him toe the mark insofar as our exalted vision is concerned. Maybe our vision isn't as exalted as we thought.

I think there are some who have seen me somehow standing on the mountain peak and hauling everybody up to me. No, we are all at the same level. That is true with respect to everyone, regardless of the level; because if we are together we are together at the level where you are. So, many peculiar notions with respect to me can dissolve on this basis. I am at the level where you are. If we proceed in our awakening we may come to the peak one day, and then that will be the level where we all are; but insofar as you are concerned, anyone is concerned, that is not now the state of affairs. So we move together. A guide wouldn't be very much good if he were standing on the top of the mountain and shouting down to those who were coming up. No, we all go through the same process together. As you awaken on the level to which you come, you find that I am there. I seem to remember something said with respect to the Lord in this regard, in the Psalms: wherever the person was, the Lord was there. This is the way it works. It is even so at the bottom. We come to see that there really is no separation between God and man except that human beings thought there was; it isn't the fact of the matter at all.

We let the awakening come naturally, and it comes because of response, that mysterious response. Many have looked upon response as simply being a conscious attitude. A conscious attitude may be included, but if that is all the response there is, woe unto you. Response, to be real, needs to be working not only on the surface but at depth. If it is working at depth and not on the surface, the individual will move up the mountain and somewhere along the way there will be an awakening. If the individual responds simply on the surface and not at depth, he may start up the mountain but he won't get very far. He will slip someplace and down he will go to the bottom. It isn't a matter of the surface alone; it isn't just a matter of your surface consciousness; there must be depth. We have had those who have been moving along apparently with us, some for quite some considerable time, whose response was evidently of that surface nature, and then suddenly, surprisingly – to many, at least – the individual vanishes from the scene.

I recall our Master spoke of the seed being sown in different places and what happened. This happens in experience. There must be a depth to the soil or it doesn't work. It may seem to for a while, but everything proves itself out. We don't have to judge; we don't have to try to make people be anything. They will be whatever they are on the basis of their response. When there is a depth of response and a surface response, then there we have something that allows for rapid awakening, a rapid movement from level to level on the mountainside. We are conscious of the movement, not because we become aware of some heavenly glory someplace but because we become aware of a different outlook on everything that is around us. We see it all with a new perspective, and this is the evidence of our movement, of our awakening, as we come to new levels of consciousness and understanding on the mountainside.

I think this is a very different state of affairs from what most human beings have imagined. You see, we lose our self-centeredness. We don't swell up with an increasing sense of greatness. Usually this is the human expectation, to become a sage, or a master, or something of the sort – to swell up like the frog. No, we lose our self-centeredness but the encompassment of our vision and understanding increases. Because of that, we do not feel any bigger; we merely have this new outlook. When the vision is complete, three hundred and sixty degrees, we are at the apex where we belong, but completely un-selfconscious.

While these things may be touched upon in our consideration, let us remember that we are presently somewhere on the side of the mountain, and while we may recognize that there is a peak, the process of awakening must continue if we are ever to find it. We stay humble, conscious of our lack of vision. And we are conscious of the lack of vision in others but, because of our own, we don't look down upon them. We are there at the level where anybody is, to provide what is needed at that level for the next awakening. We do not condemn others for being at some certain level. That's where they are; why condemn them? They couldn't be anywhere else, could they? But there is something we may do, according to response. There is that mysterious element involved all the time. Those who have response will be guided and will move and will awaken. What a very simple thing it really is; we awaken according to our response. And if we find ourselves upon the side of the mountain with a new outlook, a new perspective, then we know there must have been response. It was response to God that brought us there; not our own effort, not our own struggle, not our own mountaineering skills – just response.

So we rise up, and because we rise up we awaken. And we rise up some more and we awaken again. And level succeeds level, so that the completeness begins to come within the range of our awareness. We do not see that completeness yet but we are sure that it is there. We are sure that it is there not because we have some blind faith but because we have the experience of moving from level to level on the mountainside. We have the experience of the changing vision, the new outlook. Woe unto those who have seen something and imagine that they have seen enough. The awakening must continue, that there may be those who come to the mountaintop, which includes all the seven levels. Seeing that it includes all the seven levels, one is then present at any level where anyone may be. This is what makes true service possible.

EPILOGUE

There is an increasing response to the quality of spirit exemplified in the words of this book. The people who have indicated a desire to live in close harmony with this spirit come from every educational, economic and racial element of the world society.

This growing company regard themselves as part of a living organism and have no interest in cultivating yet another human organization. If you, after having read this book, would like to learn more about the emerging organism, you may do so by writing to:

> Director
> P.O. Box 328
> Loveland, CO 80537
> USA